# HOW TO START
# A
# BUSINESS
# IN
# MASSACHUSETTS

Julia K. O'Neill
Mark Warda
*Attorneys at Law*

Fourth Edition

SPHINX® PUBLISHING
AN IMPRINT OF SOURCEBOOKS, INC.®
NAPERVILLE, ILLINOIS
www.SphinxLegal.com

Fourth Edition: 2004
Second Printing: March, 2005

Sphinx® Publishing, a imprint of Sourcebooks, Inc.®

Naperville Office
P.O. Box 4410
Naperville, Illinois 60567-4410
630-961-3900
Fax: 630-961-2168
www.sourcebooks.com
www.SphinxLegal.com

This publication is designed to provide accurate and authoritative information in regard to the subject matter covered. It is sold with the understanding that the publisher is not engaged in rendering legal, accounting, or other professional service. If legal advice or other expert assistance is required, the services of a competent professional person should be sought.

*From a Declaration of Principles Jointly Adopted by a Committee of the American Bar Association and a Committee of Publishers and Associations*

**This product is not a substitute for legal advice.**

*Disclaimer required by Texas statutes.*

**Library of Congress Cataloging-in-Publication Data**
O'Neill, Julia K.
  How to start a business in Massachusetts / by Julia K. O'Neill.-- 4th ed.
    p. cm.
  Includes index.
  ISBN 1-57248-466-7 (alk. paper)
  1.  New business enterprises--Law and legislation--Massachusetts--Popular works.  I. Title.
KFM2552.Z9O54 2004
346.744'065--dc22
                                              2004004765

Printed and bound in the United States of America.
DR — 10  9  8  7  6  5  4  3  2

# Contents

# USING SELF-HELP LAW BOOKS

Before using a self-help law book, you should realize the advantages and disadvantages of doing your own legal work and understand the challenges and diligence that this requires.

**The Growing Trend** Rest assured that you won't be the first or only person handling your own legal matter. For example, in some states, more than seventy-five percent of the people in divorces and other cases represent themselves. Because of the high cost of legal services, this is a major trend and many courts are struggling to make it easier for people to represent themselves. However, some courts are not happy with people who do not use attorneys and refuse to help them in any way. For some, the attitude is, "Go to the law library and figure it out for yourself."

We write and publish self-help law books to give people an alternative to the often complicated and confusing legal books found in most law libraries. We have made the explanations of the law as simple and easy to understand as possible. Of course, unlike an attorney advising an individual client, we cannot cover every conceivable possibility.

**Cost/Value Analysis**

Whenever you shop for a product or service, you are faced with various levels of quality and price. In deciding what product or service to buy, you make a cost/value analysis on the basis of your willingness to pay and the quality you desire.

When buying a car, you decide whether you want transportation, comfort, status, or sex appeal. Accordingly, you decide among such choices as a Neon, a Lincoln, a Rolls Royce, or a Porsche. Before making a decision, you usually weigh the merits of each option against the cost.

When you get a headache, you can take a pain reliever (such as aspirin) or visit a medical specialist for a neurological examination. Given this choice, most people, of course, take a pain reliever, since it costs only pennies; whereas a medical examination costs hundreds of dollars and takes a lot of time. This is usually a logical choice because it is rare to need anything more than a pain reliever for a headache. But in some cases, a headache may indicate a brain tumor and failing to see a specialist right away can result in complications. Should everyone with a headache go to a specialist? Of course not, but people treating their own illnesses must realize that they are betting on the basis of their cost/value analysis of the situation. They are taking the most logical option.

The same cost/value analysis must be made when deciding to do one's own legal work. Many legal situations are very straight forward, requiring a simple form and no complicated analysis. Anyone with a little intelligence and a book of instructions can handle the matter without outside help.

But there is always the chance that complications are involved that only an attorney would notice. To simplify the law into a book like this, several legal cases often must be condensed into a single sentence or paragraph. Otherwise, the book would be several hundred pages long and too complicated for most people. However, this simplification necessarily leaves out many details and nuances that would apply to special or unusual situations. Also, there are many ways to interpret most legal questions. Your case may come before a judge who disagrees with the analysis of our authors.

Therefore, in deciding to use a self-help law book and to do your own legal work, you must realize that you are making a cost/value analysis. You have decided that the money you will save in doing it yourself outweighs the chance that your case will not turn out to your satisfaction. Most people handling their own simple legal matters never have a problem, but occasionally people find that it ended up costing them more to have an attorney straighten out the situation than it would have if they had hired an attorney in the beginning. Keep this in mind while handling your case, and be sure to consult an attorney if you feel you might need further guidance.

**Local Rules**

The next thing to remember is that a book which covers the law for the entire nation, or even for an entire state, cannot possibly include every procedural difference of every jurisdiction. Whenever possible, we provide the exact form needed; however, in some areas, each county, or even each judge, may require unique forms and procedures. In our state books, our forms usually cover the majority of counties in the state, or provide examples of the type of form which will be required. In our national books, our forms are sometimes even more general in nature but are designed to give a good idea of the type of form that will be needed in most locations. Nonetheless, keep in mind that your state, county, or judge may have a requirement, or use a form, that is not included in this book.

You should not necessarily expect to be able to get all of the information and resources you need solely from within the pages of this book. This book will serve as your guide, giving you specific information whenever possible and helping you to find out what else you will need to know. This is just like if you decided to build your own backyard deck. You might purchase a book on how to build decks. However, such a book would not include the building codes and permit requirements of every city, town, county, and township in the nation; nor would it include the lumber, nails, saws, hammers, and other materials and tools you would need to actually build the deck. You would use the book as your guide, and then do some work and research involving such matters as whether you need a permit of some kind, what type and grade of wood are available in your area, whether to use hand tools or power tools, and how to use those tools.

Before using the forms in a book like this, you should check with your court clerk to see if there are any local rules of which you should be aware, or local forms you will need to use. Often, such forms will require the same information as the forms in the book but are merely laid out differently or use slightly different language. They will sometimes require additional information.

**Changes in the Law**

Besides being subject to local rules and practices, the law is subject to change at any time. The courts and the legislatures of all fifty states are constantly revising the laws. It is possible that while you are reading this book, some aspect of the law is being changed.

In most cases, the change will be of minimal significance. A form will be redesigned, additional information will be required, or a waiting period will be extended. As a result, you might need to revise a form, file an extra form, or wait out a longer time period; these types of changes will not usually affect the outcome of your case. On the other hand, sometimes a major part of the law is changed, the entire law in a particular area is rewritten, or a case that was the basis of a central legal point is overruled. In such instances, your entire ability to pursue your case may be impaired.

Again, you should weigh the value of your case against the cost of an attorney and make a decision as to what you believe is in your best interest.

# INTRODUCTION

Each year, thousands of new corporations and limited liability companies are registered in Massachusetts and thousands more partnerships and proprietorships open for business. Entrepreneurship is alive and well in Massachusetts. From restaurants to shopping services to indoor golf courses, the new businesses just keep growing.

The best way to take part in this boom is to run your own business. Be your own boss and be as successful as you dare to be. But if you do not follow the laws of the state, your progress can be slowed or stopped by government fines, civil judgments, or even criminal penalties.

This book is intended to give you the framework for legally opening a business in Massachusetts. It also includes information on where to find special rules for each type of business. If you have problems that are not covered by this book, you should consult an attorney who can be available for your ongoing needs.

In order to cover all of the aspects of any business you are thinking of starting, you should read through this entire book, rather than skipping to the parts that look most interesting. There are many laws that may not sound like they apply to you, but that do have provisions that will affect your business.

The forms included in this book were the most recent available at the time of publication. It is possible that some may be revised by the time you read this book. Always check with the secretary of state or other appropriate authority to be sure you are using the latest forms.

Good luck with your new business!

# I | DECIDING TO START A BUSINESS

If you are reading this book, you have probably made the serious decision to take the plunge and start your own business. Hundreds of thousands of people make the same decision each year and many of them become very successful. Some merely eke out a living, others become billionaires, but a lot of them also fail. Knowledge can only help your chances of success. You need to know why some succeed while others fail. Some of what follows may seem obvious, but to someone wrapped up in a new business idea, some of this information is occasionally overlooked.

## Know Your Strengths

The last thing a budding entrepreneur wants to hear is that he or she is not cut out for running his or her own business. Those *do you have what it takes* quizzes are ignored with the fear that the answer might be one the entrepreneur does not want to hear. But even if you lack some skills, you can be successful if you know where to get them.

You should consider all of the skills and knowledge necessary to run a successful business and decide if you have what it takes. If you do not, it does not necessarily mean you are doomed to be an employee all your life. Perhaps you just need a partner who has the skills you lack. Perhaps you can hire the skills you need or can structure your business to avoid areas where you are weak. If those options do not work, maybe you can learn the skills.

For example, if you are not good at dealing with employees (either you are too passive and get taken advantage of or too tough and scare them off), you can:

✪ handle product development yourself and have a partner or manager deal with employees;

✪ take seminars in employee management; or,

✪ structure your business so that you do not need employees. Either use independent contractors or set yourself up as an independent contractor.

Here are some of the factors to consider when planning your business.

✪ *If it takes months or years before your business turns a profit, do you have the resources to stay afloat?* Businesses have gone under or been sold just before they were about to succeed. Staying power is an important ingredient to success.

✪ *Are you willing to put in a lot of overtime to make your business a success?* Owners of businesses do not set their own hours—the business sets the hours for the owner. Many business owners work long hours, seven days a week, but they enjoy running their business more than family picnics or fishing.

✪ *Are you willing to do the dirtiest or most unpleasant work of the business?* Emergencies come up and employees are not always dependable. You might need to mop up a flooded room, spend a weekend stuffing 10,000 envelopes, or work Christmas if someone calls in sick.

✪ *Do you know enough about the product or service? Are you aware of the trends in the industry and what changes new technology might bring?* Think of the people who started typesetting or printing businesses just before type was replaced by laser printers.

✪ *Do you know enough about accounting and inventory to manage the business?* Some people naturally know how to save money and do things profitably. Others are in the habit of buying the best and the most expensive of everything. The latter can be fatal to a struggling new business.

✪ *Are you good at managing employees?* While you can start a business on your own, it is usually difficult to *grow* the business without the help of additional employees. Hiring compatible and competent help is essential to your success.

✪ *Do you know how to sell your product or service?* You can have the best product on the market, but people are not beating a path to your door. If you are a wholesaler, shelf space in major stores is hard to get, especially for a new company without a record, a large line of products, or a large advertising budget.

✪ *Do you know enough about getting publicity?* The media receive thousands of press releases and announcements each day and most are thrown away. Do not count on free publicity to put your name in front of the public.

# Know Your Business

You do not only need to know the concept of a business; you need the experience of working in a business. Maybe you always dreamed of running a bed and breakfast or having your own pizza place, and now that you are laid off you think it is time to use your savings to fulfill your dream. Have you ever worked in such a business? If not, you may have no idea of the day-to-day headaches and problems of the business. For example, do you really know how much to allow for theft, spoilage, and unhappy customers?

You might feel silly taking an entry level job at a pizza place when you would rather start your own, but it might be the most valuable preparation you could have. A few weeks of seeing how a business operates could mean the difference between success and failure.

Working in a business as an employee is one of the best ways to be a success at running such a business. New people with new ideas who work in old stodgy industries have been known to revolutionize them with obvious improvements that no one ever dared to try.

# Do the Math

Conventional wisdom says you need a business plan before committing yourself to a new venture, but a lot of businesses are started successfully without the owner even knowing what a business plan is. They have a great concept, put it on the market, and it takes off. But you at least need to do some basic calculations to see if the business can make a profit. The following are some examples.

✪ If you want to start a retail shop, determine how many people are close enough to become customers and how many other stores will be competing for those customers. Visit some of those other shops and see how busy they are. Without giving away your plans to compete, ask some general questions like *how's business?* and maybe they will share their frustrations or successes.

✪ Whether you sell goods or services, do the math to find out how much profit is in it. For example, if you plan to start a house painting company, find out what you will have to pay to hire painters; what it will cost you for all of the insurance, bonding, and licensing you will need; and what the advertising will cost you. Determine how many jobs you can do per month and what other painters are charging. In some industries in different areas of the country, there may be a large margin of profit or there may be almost no profit.

✪ Find out if there is a demand for your product or service. Suppose you have designed a beautiful new kind of candle and your friends all say you should open a shop because *everyone will want them.* Before making a hundred of them and renting a store, bring a few to craft shows or flea markets and see what happens.

✪ Calculate what the income and expenses would be for a typical month of your new business. List monthly expenses such as rent, salaries, utilities, insurance, taxes, supplies, advertising, services, and other overhead.

Then figure out how much profit you will average from each sale. It is important to estimate how many sales you will need to cover your overhead and divide that number by the number of business days in the month. Can you reasonably expect that many sales? How will you get those sales?

Most types of businesses have trade associations, which often have figures on how profitable its members are. Some even have *start-up kits* for people wanting to open businesses. One good source of information on such organizations is the Encyclopedia of Associations published by Gale Research Inc. It is available in many library reference sections. Producers of products to the trade often give assistance to small companies getting started to win their loyalty. Contact the largest suppliers of the products your business will be using and see if they can be of help.

# Sources of Further Guidance

The following offices offer free or low cost guidance for new businesses.

*Small Business Administration.* Provides information on starting, financing, and expanding a business. Call 617-565-5590 or visit their website at **www.sba.gov/regions/states/ma**.

*National Association for the Self-Employed.* A 300,000-member group of small-business owners tracking legislative activities, stimulating and encouraging grass-roots businesses, and providing members with educational opportunities and health benefits. Call 800-232-6273 or visit their website at **www.nase.org**.

*Business Resource Center.* Provides information for small businesses on getting started, marketing, management, financing, etc. Visit their website at **www.morebusiness.com**.

***SCORE*** *Service Corps of Retired Executives.* Retired business executives volunteer their time to share their management and technical expertise with present and prospective owners and managers of small businesses.

**Beverly**
Danvers Savings Bank
181 Eliot Street
100 Cummings Center, Suite 101K
Beverly, MA 01915
978-927-2282

**Boston**
10 Causeway Street, Room 265
Boston, MA 02222-1093
617-565-5591

**Brockton**
60 School Street
Brockton, MA 02301
508-587-2673

**Cape Cod**
270 Communications Way, Suite 5-B
Hyannis, MA 02601
508-775-4884

**Springfield**
One Federal Street
Springfield, MA 01103
413-785-0314

**Worcester**
Worcester Regional Chamber of Commerce
339 Main Street
Worcester, MA 01608
508-753-2929

Visit their website at **www.sba.gov/regions/states/ma/score.html**.

**Massachusetts Development Centers**

*Massachusetts Department of Business and Technology.* The Massachusetts Department of Business and Technology provides a variety of information for a new business. It also provides links to other agency resources off its website at **www.state.ma.us/econ**.

*Massachusetts Department of Economic Development.* The Department of Economic Development is a state agency responsible for job creation and economic development in Massachusetts. Call 617-727-8380.

*Massachusetts Office of Business Development.* The Office of Business Development is a division of the Department of Economic Development. This office provides financial, technical, informational, and various other types of assistance to businesses in Massachusetts. Call 800-5-CAPITAL or 617-973-8600. You can also call the regional offices in the following list.

| | |
|---|---|
| Greater Boston Region: | 617-973-8686 |
| Central Region (Worcester): | 508-792-7506 |
| Northeast Region (Lowell): | 978-970-1193 |
| Southeast Region (Dartmouth): | 508-997-1438 |
| Western Region (Springfield): | 413-784-1580 |

**SOMWBA**  *The State Office of Minority and Women's Business Assistance.* SOMWBA is located within the Massachusetts Department of Economic Development. This agency promotes the development of certified minority business enterprises, women-owned business enterprises, and minority non-profit and women's non-profit organizations. Call 617-973-8692 or visit their website at **www.somwba.state.ma.us**.

**Corporation Development**  *The Commonwealth Corporation.* The Commonwealth Corporation is a government-sponsored entity that provides services to business owners and employees to promote economic growth in Massachusetts. Call 617-727-8158 or visit their website at **www.commcorp.org**.

**Small Business Development Centers**  *Massachusetts Technology Development Corporation.* The Technology Development Corporation provides funding for start-up and expansion of early-stage technology companies operating in Massachusetts. Call 617-723-4920 or visit their website at **www.mtdc.com**.

*Massachusetts Small Business Development Centers.* Small Business Development Centers stem from a program sponsored by a consortium of colleges and universities, providing management, technical assistance counseling, and educational programs to small businesses.

State Office:  413-545-6301

Counseling Centers:

| | |
|---|---|
| Boston College SBDC: | 617-552-4091 |
| Clark University SBDC: | 508-793-7615 |
| Export Center: | 617-973-8664 |
| Procurement Technical Assistance Center: | 413-545-6303 |
| Salem State College SBDC: | 978-542-6343 |

| Southeastern Mass. Regional SBDC: | 508-673-9783 |
| U Mass Boston SBDC and | 617-287-7750 |
|   Minority Business Center: | |
| Western Mass. Regional Office: | 413-737-6712 |

Or, visit their website at **msbdc.som.umass.edu**.

*Massachusetts Alliance for Economic Development.* The Massachusetts Alliance for Economic Development is a private, nonprofit corporation dedicated to fostering economic growth in Massachusetts. It provides free, customized information relating to facility relocation and expansion. Call 781-489-6262 or visit their website at **www.massecon.com**.

*Boston Entrepreneurs' Network.* The Boston Entrepreneurs' Network provides resources for starting and building businesses. Call 617-325-9852 or visit their website at **www.boston-enet.org**.

*Worcester Area Chamber of Commerce.* The Worcester Area Chamber of Commerce is the largest Chamber of Commerce in New England. It provides many networking opportunities and more. Call 508-753-2924 or visit their website at **www.worcesterchamber.org**.

*Cambridge Business Development Center.* The Business Development Center in Cambridge provides resources and support for emerging businesses, including counseling, referrals, and sponsored events. Call 617-349-4690 or visit their website at **www.cbdc.org**.

*Foundation for Continuing Education.* The Foundation for Continuing Education is a nonprofit educational resource that presents seminars and publishes books in the areas of finance, estate and business planning, taxes, business development, and computer programming. Call 978-468-6528 or visit their website at **www.fce.org**.

*The Enterprise Center at Salem State College.* The Enterprise Center is a mixed-use business park with space available to established and start-up companies. On-site support services, business incubator program, and an entrepreneurs' network to help new and emerging businesses on the North Shore. Call 978-542-7528 or visit their website at **www.enterprisectr.org**.

# 2 | Choosing the Form of Your Business

The six most common forms of business entities in Massachusetts are proprietorship, partnership, corporation, limited partnership, limited liability company, and limited liability partnership. Some of the characteristics, advantages, and disadvantages of each are described in this chapter.

## Proprietorship

A *proprietorship* is one person doing business in his or her own name or under a *fictitious name*.

**Advantages**      Simplicity is just one of the many advantages. Others include no organizational expense, no extra tax forms, and no reports.

**Disadvantages**      The proprietor is personally liable for all debts and obligations. There is no continuation of the business after death. All profits are directly taxable, certainly a disadvantage for the proprietor, and business affairs are too easily mixed with personal affairs.

# General Partnership

A *general partnership* involves two or more people carrying on a business together and sharing the profits and losses.

***Advantages***  Partners can combine expertise and assets. A general partnership allows liability to be spread among more persons. Also, the business can be continued after the death of a partner if bought out by the surviving partner.

***Disadvantages***  Each partner is liable for acts of other partners within the scope of the business. This means that if your partner harms a customer or signs a million-dollar credit line in the partnership name, you can be personally liable. All profits are taxable, even if left in the business.

Control is shared by all parties and the death of a partner may result in liquidation. In a general partnership, it is often hard to get rid of a bad partner.

# Corporation

A *corporation* is an artificial *legal person* that carries on business through its officers and directors, for its shareholders. (In Massachusetts, one person may form a corporation and be the sole shareholder, director, and officer.) The corporation carries on business in its own name and shareholders are usually not liable for its acts. As of July 1, 2004, laws covering most business corporations are contained in Massachusetts General Laws (Mass. Gen. Laws), Chapter (Ch.) 156D. This new act supersedes Chapter 156B.

In a corporation, the *shareholders* elect the directors. The directors then elect the officers. In Massachusetts, the law until June 30, 2004 requires that if the corporation had three or fewer shareholders, it must have at least the same number of directors. As of July 1, 2004, a corporation may avoid this rule (*e.g.*, have any number of directors regardless of the number of shareholders) by providing otherwise in its articles of organization. The officers have authority to run the day-to-day operations, but they need directors' approval to do anything out of the ordinary, such as sign a lease for business space, hire an executive employee, or start a new line of business. For even more major decisions, such as sale of all or substantially all of the assets of the corporation, merger, reorganization, consolidation, or amendment to the articles of organization, a shareholders' vote is required.

An *amendment* to the articles of organization is required in order to increase the number of authorized shares of stock, add another class or series of stock (unless a bank of undesignated shares has been previously authorized in the articles), change the corporation's name, and to take various other actions. In Massachusetts, a majority shareholder vote is required to authorize certain amendments to the articles of organization, including a change of the corporation's name or a stock split. For more major matters, such as merger, consolidation, or sale of all or substantially all of the assets, a two-thirds vote is required, unless the company's articles of organization provide for a lesser vote.

**Types**  *S corporation.* An *S corporation* is a corporation that has filed IRS Form 2553, choosing to have all profits taxed to, and other tax attributes flow through to, the shareholders rather than to the corporation. An S corporation files a tax return but pays no federal tax. The profits (or losses) shown on the S corporation tax return are reported on the owners' tax returns. In Massachusetts, even an S corporation must pay the minimum state excise tax of $456 per year.

Generally, to elect S corporation status, the following conditions must be satisfied:

✪  the corporation must be a U.S. corporation;

✪  there must be no more than seventy-five shareholders;

✪  shareholders may only be individuals, estates, specified types of trusts, or certain exempt organizations; and,

✪  only one class of stock is allowed, although the voting rights can differ.

*C corporation.* A *C corporation* is any business corporation that has not elected to be taxed as an S corporation. A C corporation pays both state and federal income tax on its profits. The effect of having business profits taxed at the corporate level, unlike the S corporation, is that the profits are taxed twice—once at the corporate level (as income to the corporation) and a second time at the shareholder level (as dividend income to the shareholder).

*Professional corporation.* A *professional corporation* is a corporation formed by a professional such as a doctor or accountant. Massachusetts has special rules for professional corporations that differ slightly from those of other corporations. These rules are included in Chapter 156A of the Massachusetts General Laws. A professional corporation may be an S corporation.

Massachusetts laws require a majority of the directors and all of the officers other than treasurer, secretary, assistant treasurer, and assistant secretary of a professional corporation to be a licensed practitioners of the profession that the corporation has been organized to practice. When filing the organizational documents, the incorporators of a professional corporation have to obtain proof from the appropriate licensing board that the necessary persons are duly licensed.

In addition, Massachusetts law prohibits the issuance or transfer of shares to a person who is not professionally licensed. The various licensing boards also often have authority, by statute, to promulgate additional requirements with which professional corporations must comply.

*Nonprofit corporation.* A *nonprofit corporation* is usually used for organizations such as churches and condominium associations. However, with careful planning, some types of businesses can be set up as nonprofit corporations and save a fortune in taxes. While a nonprofit corporation cannot pay dividends, it can pay its officers and employees fair salaries. Some of the major American nonprofit organizations pay their officers well over $100,000 a year. Massachusetts' special rules for nonprofit corporations are included in Chapter 180 of the Massachusetts General Laws.

**Advantages**    If a corporation is properly organized and maintained, shareholders have no liability for corporate debts and lawsuits. Also, officers and directors usually have no personal liability for their corporate acts. The existence of a corporation may be perpetual, that is, it will survive changes in owners. There are tax advantages allowed only to corporations. There is prestige in owning a corporation.

Capital may be raised by issuing stock and it is fairly easy to transfer ownership upon death. A small corporation can be set up as an S corporation to avoid corporate taxes but still retain corporate advantages, such as limited liability. Some types of businesses can be set up as nonprofit corporations, which provide significant tax savings.

**Disadvantages**    There are start-up costs for forming a corporation. Plus there are certain formalities that must be followed, such as annual meetings, separate bank accounts, and special tax forms. Unless a corporation registers as an S corporation, it must pay federal income tax separate from the tax paid by the owners and may pay more than the minimum state excise tax.

# Limited Partnership

A *limited partnership* has characteristics similar to both a corporation and a partnership. There are *general partners* who have the control and personal liability, and there are *limited partners* who only put up money and whose liability is limited to what they paid for their share of the partnership (like corporate stock).

**Advantages**

*Capital* can be contributed by limited partners who have no control of the business or liability for its debts.

**Disadvantages**

A great disadvantage is high start-up costs. Also, an extensive partnership agreement is required because general partners are personally liable for partnership debts and for the acts of each other. (One solution to this problem is to use a corporation as the general partner.)

# Limited Liability Company

Massachusetts was one of the last states to allow the formation of a limited liability company. Previously, Massachusetts required LLCs to have at least two members. Fortunately, this law was recently changed so that now one-member LLCs are allowed. As an alternative to the corporate form, the LLC is steadily gaining in popularity. This entity is like a limited partnership without general partners. It has characteristics of both a corporation and a partnership. None of the members have liability and all can have some control. It does not have to be taxed for federal purposes at the company level but can choose to be taxed like a partnership (unless it has only one member, in which case it will be taxed like a sole proprietorship).

**Advantages**

The limited liability company offers the tax benefits of a partnership (if the entity chooses to be taxed as a partnership rather than a corporation) with the protection from liability of a corporation. It offers more tax benefits and flexibility than an S corporation because it may pass through more depreciation and deductions. Allocations of income, gain, loss, deduction, and credit can be made in proportions that are different than the equity owners' respective ownership interests, subject to various limitations.

It may have different classes of ownership, an unlimited number of members, and aliens as members. If it owns appreciated property, it has more favorable tax treatment upon dissolution than an S corporation. The limited liability company is also extremely flexible in structure and operational aspects, since those are not dictated strictly by statute as they are for corporations.

**Disadvantages**     There are higher start-up costs than for a corporation. Due to the flexibility in structural and operational aspects, the governing documents are more complex and expensive to have properly prepared than those of a corporation. The LLC may also be subject to personal property tax on inventory in Massachusetts to which a corporation would not be subject.

# Limited Liability Partnership

The limited liability partnership is like a general partnership but without personal liability. It was devised to allow partnerships of lawyers and other professionals limit their personal liability without losing their partnership structure.

**NOTE:** *The law does not allow professionals to limit their liability for negligence in their own professional functions,* i.e., *malpractice.*

This was important because converting to an LLC could have tax consequences, and some states do not allow professionals to operate as LLCs. Both general and limited partnerships can register as LLPs.

**Advantages**     The LLP offers the flexibility and tax benefits of a partnership with the protection from liability of a corporation.

**Disadvantages**     Start-up and annual fees are higher for limited liability partnerships than for a corporation.

# Massachusetts S Corporations versus Massachusetts LLCs

Often the start up will narrow down its choices of entity to two—the S corporation and the LLC. Both entities will protect the principals from any personal liability for the business's debts and obligations, assuming formalities are followed and no circumstances lend themselves to a creditor's being able to *pierce the corporate veil*. Both entities also have their income taxed to the principals on a pass-through basis, such that there is no tax at the entity level, but only at the individual owner level. However, the S corporation must pay an annual minimum excise tax of $456 to the Commonwealth of Massachusetts. If an S corporation's annual receipts exceed six million dollars, the entity could become liable for substantial state income taxes. The LLC is not liable for any state excise tax.

Different circumstances may point to a choice of one type of entity or another. There are always pros and cons to both choices. But being aware of the differences and similarities between these two types of entities will help you to make the right choice.

**Filing Fees**

The cost of the annual filing fee for the LLC makes up for the lack of excise tax liability. The fee for filing an LLC's annual report with the secretary of state is $500, while the S corporation's annual filing fee is $125. The initial filing fees for forming the entities are $500 for an LLC and $275 (minimum, depending on the amount of stock authorized) for the S corporation. Thus, while the initial fees differ by $225, the annual fees for upkeep for the two types of entities are substantially similar.

**Restrictions On Transfer**

Both the LLC and the S corporation lend themselves easily to restrictions on transfer to protect the principals from having outsiders as co-owners. The LLC's operating agreement can include these restrictions on transfer and buy-sell provisions. The shares in an S corporation can be made subject to such provisions by their inclusion in the articles of organization or by contract.

Some practitioners and business people assume that *newer is better*. They automatically choose the LLC over the S corporation because the LLC is new, more modern, and therefore, must be better. As when you choose a computer or a word-processing program, you should evaluate how you plan to use it, what you plan to do with it in the future, and other various implications of the choice in order to select the model that is right for you.

**Statutes**
The structure and function of the S corporation are governed by statute. With the recent change in the corporations law in Massachusetts, the private corporation now can be governed with almost as much flexibility as an LLC. The new law allows the corporation to dispense with the Board of Directors entirely, make distributions disproportionate to stock ownership, delegate authority in a broader manner, and change other governing provisions, as long as the change is not contrary to public policy. However, the LLC still carries many more choices than the S corporation with respect to setup, operation, and termination.

Although flexibility can be a bonus, it carries with it a certain level of complexity that some people would rather avoid. The flexibility that comes with an LLC necessarily involves decision-making, which some may find daunting.

In making this decision, you should also consider whether your business is likely to ever go public. If so, an LLC will not work. The business could, however, convert from an LLC to a corporation prior to going public, with not too much trouble or tax consequence.

**Owners/ Members**
Another major difference between the LLC and the S corporation relates to the number and type of owners or members. In Massachusetts, there are no restrictions on how many members an LLC may have or who they may be (*e.g.*, individuals, corporations, or other entities). The S corporation may have as few as one shareholder but no more than seventy-five (husband and wife are treated as one), and they must meet certain criteria. They must be individuals, estates, certain types of trusts, or certain exempt organizations, and they may not be nonresident aliens. The S corporation can only have one class of stock (although differences solely in voting rights are allowed). The LLC can have many different types of owners and equity interests in one entity.

**Taxes**
Although the tax treatment of the two types of entities is generally similar (*i.e.*, tax attributes flow through to the equity owner level and there is no entity-level tax), there are some differences which should be considered.

One tax aspect to consider is that the income of an LLC that flows through to persons involved with the business will generally be subject to self-employment tax. With an S corporation, only salaries are subject to self-employment tax. If other income is paid out as S corporation distributions, it will not be subject to self-employment tax.

**NOTE:** *In this regard, the IRS has broad authority to characterize income as it sees fit.*

A second tax difference between the two entities is that in an LLC, distributions of appreciated property will generally be tax free, and the members will have a carry over basis in the distributed assets. Not so with an S corporation. Distributed appreciated assets will cause shareholders in an S corporation to have taxable income and take a basis of current fair market value in the assets. This is the major reason that conversion from an S corporation to an LLC creates tax issues, while conversion from an LLC to an S corporation generally does not.

A third, and very important, tax difference is that in the LLC, owners generally can have different allocations of tax benefits, like depreciation and losses, without regard to their *pro rata* ownership interests. The S corporation cannot make special allocations of these tax items.

There can be a major tax problem for Massachusetts LLCs that carry inventory. The personal property tax statutes specifically exempt personal property of domestic business corporations, but not of LLCs. This means that an LLC with substantial personal property (*e.g.*, inventory such as automobiles) will be liable for property tax that the business would not have been liable for had it been formed as a corporation. This legislative omission could be a costly trap for some businesses.

The LLC is generally preferable to the S corporation when the entity will own real estate subject to substantial debt because the LLC provides the benefit of member-level tax basis adjustments for LLC liabilities and the allowance of an adjustment in the tax basis of the entity's assets upon the sale of a member's interest. The S corporation shareholder cannot include any part of the corporation's debt in the tax basis of his or her stock, unless he or she loaned the money to the corporation. Because of these differences, LLC members are able to deduct more of the entity's tax losses as they occur than S corporation shareholders.

# Start-Up Procedures

For those entities that are required to make filings with the secretary of state, the Corporations Division's website has loads of information and forms. It is located at **www.sec.state.ma.us/cor/coridx.htm**.

**Proprietorship**   In a proprietorship, all accounts, property, and licenses are taken in the name of the owner. (See Chapter 3 for using a fictitious name.)

***Partnership***     To form a partnership, a written agreement should be prepared to spell out rights and obligations of the parties. (See Chapter 3 for using a fictitious name.) Most accounts, property, and licenses can be in either the partnership name or that of the partners.

***Corporation***     To form a corporation, articles of organization must be filed with the secretary of state in Boston, along with a minimum filing fee of $275. An organizational meeting is then held at which officers are elected, stock issued, and other formalities observed. If these formalities are not followed, you risk the possibility of a creditor being able to *pierce the corporate veil*, or have the corporate entity set aside in order to render shareholders personally liable for the company's obligations. Contracts, licenses, accounts, and the like are in the name of the corporation.

***Limited Partnership***     A Certificate of Limited Partnership must be drawn up and registered with the secretary of state in Boston, and generally, a lengthy disclosure document must be given to all prospective limited partners. Because of the complexity of securities laws and the criminal penalties for violation, it is advantageous to have an attorney organize a limited partnership.

***Limited Liability Company***     One or more persons may form a *limited liability company* by filing a Certificate of Formation with the secretary of state in Boston. The filing fee is $500. Contracts, licenses, and accounts are in the name of the company.

***Limited Liability Partnership***     Two or more persons may form a limited liability partnership by filing a registration form with the secretary of state in Boston. The filing fee is $500. Licenses and accounts are in the name of the company.

# Required Contacts

| TYPES OF BUSINESS | AGENCY | DIVISION | TELEPHONE | REQUIREMENT | FREQUENCY |
|---|---|---|---|---|---|
| Business Corporation | Secretary of Commonwealth | Corporations | 617-727-9640 | • file Articles of Organization<br>• file Articles of Amendment<br>• file Annual Report<br>• file Articles of Dissolution | Once<br>When Necessary<br>Annually<br>Upon termination |
| Professional Corporation | Secretary of Commonwealth | Corporations | 617-727-9640 | • same as for business corporation, plus;<br>  - a certificate of the appropriate regulating board(s) that each of the incorporators, the president, and any vice presidents, a majority of the directors and each shareholder is duly licensed, must accompany Articles of Organization | Once |
| Nonprofit Corporation | Secretary of Commonwealth | Corporations | 617-727-9640 | • same as for business corporations except:<br>  - file Annual Report<br>  - dissolved through court action | Annually on November 1 |
| Foreign Corporation | Secretary of Commonwealth | Corporations | 617-727-9640 | • file Certificate of Registration<br>• file amended certificate<br>• file Annual Report<br>• file Certificate of Withdrawal | Once<br>When necessary<br>Annually<br>Upon cessation of business in the Commonwealth |
| Limited Partnership | Secretary of the Commonwealth | Corporations | 617-727-2859 | • file Certificate of Limited Partnership<br>• file amended certificate<br>• file Certificate of Cancellation | Once<br>When necessary<br>Upon dissolution |
| Foreign Limited Partnership | Secretary of the Commonwealth | Corporations | 617-727-2859 | • file Certificate of Registration<br>• file amended certificate<br>• file Certificate of Withdrawal | Once<br>When necessary<br>Upon cessation of business in the Commonwealth<br>Upon dissolution |
| Business Trust | Secretary of the Commonwealth | Corporations | 617-727-2859 | • file Declaration of trust<br>• file amended declaration<br>• file Annual Report | Once<br>When Necessary<br>Annually |
|  | Secretary of the Commonwealth | Securities Division | 617-727-3548<br>800-269-5428 | • broker/dealer registration<br>• investment advisor registration<br>• corporate finance section | When necessary<br>When necessary<br>When necessary |

*(continued on next page)*

| TYPE OF BUSINESS | AGENCY | DIVISION | TELEPHONE | REQUIREMENT | FREQUENCY |
|---|---|---|---|---|---|
| Limited Liability Companies | Secretary of the Commonwealth | Corporations | 617-727-2859 | Domestic: <br>• file Certificate of Formation <br>• file Certificate of Amendment <br>• file Annual Report <br>• file Certificate of Cancellation <br>Foreign: <br>• file Registration <br>• file Amendment <br>• file Annual Report <br>• file Certificate of Withdrawal | Once <br>When necessary <br>Annually <br>Upon dissolution <br><br>Once <br>When necessary <br>Annually <br>Upon dissolution |
| Limited Liability Partnerships | Secretary of the Commonwealth | Corporations | 617-727-2859 | Domestic and Foreign: <br>• file Certificate of Registration <br>• file Amendment Registration <br>• file Annual Report <br>• file Certificate of Withdrawal | Once <br>When necessary <br>Annually <br>Upon withdrawal of registration or dissolution |

# Business Comparison Chart

| | Sole Proprietorship | General Partnership | Limited Partnership | Limited Liability Co. | Limited Liability Partnership | Corporation C or S | Nonprofit Corporation |
|---|---|---|---|---|---|---|---|
| Liability Protection | No | No | For limited partners | For all members | For all members | For all shareholders | For all members |
| Taxes | Pass through | Pass through | Pass through | Pass through | Pass through | S corps. pass through; C corps. pay tax | None |
| Minimum # of members | 1 | 2 | 2 | 1 | 2 | 1 | 1 |
| Start-up fee | None | None | $200 | $500 | $500 | Min $275 | $35 |
| Annual fee | None | None | N/A | $500 | $500 | $125 | $15 |
| Diff. classes of ownership | No | No | Yes | Yes | Yes | S corps. No C corps. Yes | No ownership Diff. classes of membership |
| Survives after Death | No | No | Yes | Yes | No | Yes | Yes |
| Best for | 1 person low-risk business or no assets | Low-risk business | Low-risk business with silent partners | All types of businesses | Law Firms | All types of businesses | Educational |

# Business Start-Up Checklist

❑ Make your plan
  ❑ Obtain and read all relevant publications on your type of business
  ❑ Obtain and read all laws and regulations affecting your business
  ❑ Calculate whether your plan will produce a profit
  ❑ Plan your sources of capital
  ❑ Plan your sources of goods or services
  ❑ Plan your marketing efforts
❑ Choose your business name
  ❑ Check other business names and trademarks
  ❑ Register your name, trademark, etc.
❑ Choose the business form
  ❑ Prepare and file organizational papers
  ❑ Prepare and file fictitious name if necessary
❑ Choose the location
  ❑ Check competitors
  ❑ Check zoning
❑ Obtain necessary licenses
  ❑ City?              ❑ State?
  ❑ County?            ❑ Federal?
❑ Choose a bank
  ❑ Checking
  ❑ Credit card processing
  ❑ Loans
❑ Obtain necessary insurance
  ❑ Worker's Comp        ❑ Automobile
  ❑ Unemployment         ❑ Liability
  ❑ Health               ❑ Hazard
  ❑ Life/disability
❑ File necessary federal tax registrations
❑ File necessary state tax registrations
❑ Set up a bookkeeping system
❑ Plan your hiring
  ❑ Obtain required posters
  ❑ Obtain or prepare employment application
  ❑ Obtain new hire tax forms
  ❑ Prepare employment policies
  ❑ Determine compliance with health and safety laws
❑ Plan your opening
  ❑ Obtain all necessary equipment and supplies
  ❑ Obtain all necessary inventory
  ❑ Do all necessary marketing and publicity
  ❑ Obtain all necessary forms and agreements
  ❑ Prepare your company policies on refunds, exchanges, returns

# YOUR BUSINESS NAME

Before deciding on a name for your business, you should be sure that it is not already being used by someone else. Many business owners spend thousands of dollars on publicity and printing, only to throw it all away because another company owned the name. A company that owns a name can take you to court and force you to stop using that name. It can also sue you for damages if it thinks your use of the name caused it a financial loss.

If you will be running a small local shop with no plans for expansion, you should at least check out whether the name has been trademarked. If someone else is using the same name anywhere in the country and has registered it as a federal trademark, they can sue you. If you plan to expand or to deal nationally, you should do a more thorough search of the name.

## Name Searches

To search for a name you are considering using, the first places to look are the local phone books and city or town clerk's office (for a fictitious name filing). Next, you should check with the secretary of state's office in Boston to see if someone has registered a corporate or LLC name that is the same as, or confusingly similar to, the one you have chosen. The secretary of state's office can be reached at 617-727-2850 or 617-727-9640.

To do a national search, you should check trade directories and phone books of major cities. These can be found at many libraries but usually can only be used at the library and not checked out. The *Trade Names Directory* is a two volume set of names compiled from many sources and published by Gale Research Company. If you have a computer with Internet access, you can use it to search the Yellow Pages at **www.yellowpages.com.**

To be sure that your use of the name does not violate someone else's trademark rights, you should have a trademark search done in the United States Patent and Trademark Office (USPTO). In the past, this required a visit to their offices or the hiring of a search for over a hundred dollars. Now you can search the trademark records online at **www.uspto.gov.** Keep in mind that this database is not kept altogether current.

If you do not have access to the Internet, you might be able to do it on a computer at a public library or have one of their employees order an online search for a small fee. If this is not available to you, you can have the search done through a firm, such as Thomson & Thomson at **www.thomson-thomson.com** or 800-692-8833.

No matter how thorough your search, there is no guarantee that there is not a local user somewhere with rights to the mark. If, for example, you register a name for a new chain of restaurants and later find out that someone in Tucumcari, New Mexico has been using the name longer than you, that person will still have the right to use the name, but probably just in that local area. If you do not want that restaurant to cause confusion with your chain, you can offer to buy it. Similarly, if you are operating a small business under a unique name and a law firm in New York writes and offers to buy the right to your name, you can assume that some large corporation wants to start a major expansion under that name.

The best way to make sure a name you are using is not already owned by someone else is to make up a name. Names such as Xerox, Kodak, and Exxon were made up and did not have any meaning prior to their use. Remember that there are millions of businesses, so even something you make up may already be in use. Do a search to be sure.

# Fictitious Names

In Massachusetts, as in most states, unless you do business in your own legal name, you must register the business name (called a *fictitious name*) you are using. The name must be registered with the clerk of each city and town where you have an office.

A fictitious name registration is good for four years and can be renewed for additional four-year periods. Failure to make the required filings can result in fines of $300 per month.

If your name is Jennifer Anne and you are operating a fan store, you may operate your business as *Jennifer Anne, Portable Fans* without registering the name. But variations on your name, such as *Jenny Anne, the Fan Fan*, should be registered.

You cannot use the words *corporation, incorporated, corp.,* or *inc.,* unless you are a corporation. However, a corporation does not have to register the name it is using unless it is different from its registered corporate name. A partnership does not have to register the name it is using as long as it contains the surname of any partner.

Legally, when you use a fictitious name, you are *doing business as* (d/b/a) whatever name you are using. For example, *Jennifer Anne d/b/a Jenny Anne, The Fan Fan*.

As discussed in the previous section, you should do some research to see if the name you intend to use is already being used by anyone else. Even persons who have not registered a name can acquire legal rights to the name through use.

Most cities and towns have their own fictitious name form. You should call the city or town clerk and ask them to send it to you. If they do not have one, you can use the **Certificate Stating Real Name of Person Transacting Business** (form 2, p.191).

# Corporate Names

A corporation does not have to register a fictitious name unless it uses a name that is different from its true legal name. In the judgment of the secretary of state, the name of a corporation must include a word or words indicating that it is a corporation. Regulations indicate that one of the following words (or its abbreviation) will suffice:

| | |
|---|---|
| Incorporated | Inc. |
| Corporation | Corp. |
| Limited | Ltd. |
| Company | Co. |

If the name of the corporation does not contain one of the approved words, it will probably be rejected by the secretary of state. It will also be rejected if the name is already taken or is similar to the name of another corporation, or if it uses a forbidden word such as *Bank* or *Trust.* To check on a name, you may call the secretary of state at 617-727-2850.

If a name you choose is taken by another company, you may be able to change it slightly and have it accepted. For example, if there is already a Fisher Cut Bait, Inc., in a different county, you may be allowed to use Fisher Cut Bait, Inc. of Dukes County. But even if approved by the secretary of state, you may get sued by the other company if your business is close to theirs or there is a likelihood of confusion.

Also, do not have anything printed until your corporate papers are returned to you. Sometimes a name is approved over the phone and rejected when submitted.

Once you have chosen a corporate name and know it is available, you should immediately form your corporation. A name can be *reserved* for a month for $15, but it is easier just to form the corporation than to waste time on the name reservation.

If a corporation wants to do business under a name other than its corporate name, it can register a fictitious name such as *Luke the Duke of Earl, Inc., d/b/a Luke the Duke.* However, if the name used leads people to believe that the business is not a corporation, there may be some risk of losing the right to limited liability that the corporate entity provides. If such a name is used, it should always be accompanied by the corporate name.

# Professional Corporations

*Professional corporations* are corporations formed by professionals, such as attorneys, doctors, dentists, and architects. In Massachusetts, a professional corporation can use any of the usual corporate designations—Inc., Corp., and so on—or the words *Professional Corporation* or the abbreviation *P.C.*

# The Word *Limited*

The words *Limited* or *Ltd.* at the end of a name can be used for a corporation, although some people find this confusing because they associate the word with a limited partnership. The phrase *Limited Liability Company*, or its abbreviation, *L.L.C.*, should only be used if you are doing business in the form of a limited liability company.

# Domain Names

A discussion of domain names is contained in Chapter 15 of this book.

# Trademarks

As your business builds goodwill, its name will become more valuable and you will want to protect it from others who may wish to copy it. To protect a name used to describe your goods or services, you can register it as a trademark (for goods) or a service mark (for services) with either the secretary of state of Massachusetts or with the United States Patent and Trademark Office.

You cannot register a trademark for the name of your business unless that name is also the name of goods or services you are selling. In many cases, you use your company name on your goods as your trademark. In effect, it protects your company name. Another way to protect your company name is to incorporate. A unique corporate name can only be registered by one company in Massachusetts.

**State Registration**

State registration would be useful if you only expect to use your trademark within Massachusetts. Federal registration would protect your mark anywhere in the country. Use of a mark without registration does give you some legal rights to the mark, but registration of the mark gives you much better protection. The registration of a mark constitutes proof that you are the exclusive owner of the mark for the types of goods or services for which it is registered. The only exception is persons who have already been using the mark. People who have been using the mark prior to your registration may have superior rights even though they have not registered the mark.

The procedure for state registration is simple and the cost is $50. First, you should write to the secretary of state, or call 617-727-2859 to ask them to search your name and tell you if it is available. For questions about filing the application, call the same number. The secretary of state can be reached by mail at:

**Secretary of State**
Trademark Division
1 Ashburton Place
Boston, MA 02108

Before a mark can be registered, it must be used in Massachusetts. For goods, this means it must be used on the goods themselves or on containers, tags, labels, or displays of the goods. For services, it must be used in the sale or advertising of the services. The use must be in an actual transaction with a customer. A sample mailed to a friend is not considered acceptable use.

The $50 fee will register the mark in only one *class of goods*. If the mark is used on more than one class of goods, a separate registration must be filed. Three *specimens* of use of the mark must also be filed. The registration is good for ten years. It must be renewed six months prior to its expiration. The renewal fee is $50 for each class of goods.

An **APPLICATION FOR REGISTRATION OF A TRADEMARK** (form 3, p.193) is included in the back of this book. At the end of this chapter is the *Massachusetts Classification of Goods and Services* (similar, but not identical to, the federal classifications), which you will need to fill out your application.

**Federal Registration**

The procedure for federal registration is a little more complicated. There are two types of applications depending upon whether you have already made actual use of the mark or whether you merely have an intention to use the mark in the future. For a trademark that has been in use, you must file an application form along with specimens showing actual use and a drawing of the mark that complies with all of the rules of the United States Patent and Trademark Office. For an *intent to use* application, you must file two separate forms: one when you make the initial application, and the other after you have made *actual use* of the mark as well as the specimens and drawing. Before a mark can be entitled to federal registration, the use of the mark must be in *interstate commerce* or in commerce with another country. The fee for registration is $335; but if you file an *intent to use* application, there is a second fee of $100 for the filing after actual use.

For more information on federal registration and to complete an online application, visit **www.uspto.gov**.

## Massachusetts Classification of Goods

1. Chemical products used in industry, science, photography, agriculture, horticulture, forestry; artificial and synthetic resins; plastics in the form of powders, liquids or pastes, for industrial use; manures (natural and artificial); fire extinguishing compositions; tempering substances and chemical preparations for soldering; chemical substances for preserving foodstuffs; tanning substances; adhesive substance used in industry.

2. Paints, varnishes, lacquers, preservatives against rust and against deterioration of wood; coloring matters, dyestuffs; mordants; natural resins; metals in foil; and powder form for painters and decorators.

3. Bleaching preparations and other substances for laundry use; cleaning, polishing, scouring and abrasive preparations; soaps; perfumery; essential oils, cosmetics, hair lotions; and, dentifrices.

4. Industrial oils and greases (other than edible oils and fats and essential oils); lubricants; dust laying and absorbing compositions; fuels (including motor spirit) and illuminants; candles, tapers, nightlights and wicks.

5. Pharmaceutical veterinary and sanitary substances; infants' and invalids' food; plasters, material for bandaging; material for stopping teeth, dental wax; disinfectants; preparations for killing weeds and destroying vermin.

6. Unwrought and partly wrought common metals and their alloys; anchors, anvils, bells, rolled and cast building materials; rails and other metallic materials for railway tracks; chains (except driving chains for vehicles); cables and wires (nonelectric); locksmiths' work; metallic pipes and tubes; safes and cash boxes; steel balls; horseshoes; nails and screws other goods in non-precious metal included in other classes; ores.

7. Machines and machine tools; motors (except for land vehicles); machine couplings and belting (except for land vehicles); large size agricultural implements; incubators.

8. Hand tools and instruments; cutlery, forks and spoons; side arms.

9.  Scientific, nautical, surveying and electrical apparatus and instruments (including wireless), photographic, cinematographic, optical, weighing, measuring, signalling, checking (supervision), lifesaving and teaching apparatus and instruments; coin or counter-freed apparatus; talking machines; cash registers; calculating machines; fire-extinguishing apparatus.

10. Surgical, medical, dental and veterinary instruments and apparatus (including artificial limbs, eyes, and teeth).

11. Installations for lighting, heating, steam generating, cooking, refrigerating, drying, ventilating, water supply, and sanitary purposes.

12. Vehicles; apparatus for locomotion by land, air, or water.

13. Firearms; ammunition and projectiles; explosive substances; fireworks.

14. Precious metals and their alloys and goods in precious metals or coated therewith (except cutlery, forks, and spoons); jewelry, precious stones, horological and other chronometric instruments.

15. Musical instruments (other than talking machines and wireless apparatus).

16. Paper and paper articles, cardboard and cardboard articles; printed matter, newspapers and periodicals, books; binding material, photographs; stationery, adhesive materials (stationery); artists' materials; paint brushes; typewriters and office requisites (other than furniture); instructional and teaching material (other than apparatus); playing cards; printers' type and cliches (stereotype).

17. Cutta percha, india rubber, balata and substitutes, articles made from these substances and not included in other classes; plastics in the form of sheets, blocks and rods, being for use in manufacture; materials for packing, stopping or insulating; asbestos, mica and their products; hose pipes (nonmetallic).

18. Leather and imitations of leather, and articles made from these materials and not included in other classes; skins, hides; trunks and traveling bags; umbrellas, parasols and walking sticks; whips, harness and saddlery.

19. Building materials, natural and artificial stone, cement, lime, mortar, plaster and gravel; pipes of earthenware or cement; road making materials; asphalt, pitch and bitumen; portable buildings; stone monuments; chimney pots.

20. Furniture, mirrors, picture frames; articles (not included in other classes) of wood, cork, reeds, cane, wicker, horn, bone, ivory, whalebone, shell, amber, mother-of-pearl, meerschaum, celluloid, substitutes for all these materials, or of plastics.

21. Small domestic utensils and containers (not of precious metal or coated therewith); combs and sponges; brushes (other than paint brushes); brush-making materials; instruments and material for cleaning purposes; steelwool; glassware, porcelain and earthenware, not included in other classes.

22. Ropes, string, nets, tents, awnings, tarpaulins, sails, sacks; padding and stuffing materials (hair, kapok, feathers, seaweed, etc.); raw fibrous textile materials.

23. Yarns, threads.

24. Fabrics (piece goods); bed and table covers; textile articles not included in other classes.

25. Clothing, including boots, shoes and slippers.

26. Lace and embroidery, ribbons and braids; buttons, press buttons, hooks and eyes, pins and needles; artificial flowers.

27. Carpets, rugs, mats and matting; linoleum and other materials for covering floors; wall hangings (non-textile).

28. Games and playthings; gymnastics and sporting articles (except clothing); ornaments and decorations for Christmas trees.

29. Meat, fish, poultry and game; meat extracts; preserved, dried and cooked fruits and vegetables; jellies, jams, eggs, milk and other dairy products; edible oils and fats; preserves, pickles.

30. Coffee, tea, cocoa, sugar, rice, tapioca, sago, coffee substitutes; flour, and preparations made from cereals; breads, biscuits, cakes, pastry and confectionary, ices; honey, treacle; yeast, baking-powder; salt, mustard; pepper, vinegar, sauces, spices; ice.

31. Agricultural, horticultural and forestry products and grains not included in other classes; living animals; fresh fruits and vegetables; seeds; live plants and flowers; foodstuffs for animals, malt.

32. Beer, ale and porter; mineral and aerated waters and other nonalcoholic drinks; syrups and other preparations for making beverages.

33. Wine, spirits and liqueurs.

34. Tobacco, raw or manufactured; smokers' articles; matches.

## Classification of Services

35. Advertising and business.

36. Insurance and financial.

37. Construction and repair.

38. Communication.

39. Transportation and storage.

40. Material treatment.

41. Education and entertainment.

42. Miscellaneous.

# 4 FINANCING YOUR BUSINESS

The way to finance your business is determined by how fast you want your business to grow and how much risk of failure you are able to handle. Letting the business grow with its own income is the slowest but safest way to grow. Taking out a personal loan against your house to expand quickly is one of the fastest but riskiest ways to grow.

## Growing with Profits

Many successful businesses have started out with little money and used the profits to grow bigger and bigger. If you have another source of income to live on (such as a job or a spouse), you can plow all the income of your fledgling business into growth.

Some businesses start as hobbies or part time ventures on the weekend while the entrepreneur holds down a full time job. Many types of goods or service businesses can start this way. Even some multi-million dollar corporations, such as Apple Computer, started out this way.

This allows you to test your idea with little risk. If you find you are not good at running that type of business or the time or location was not right for your idea, all you have lost is the time you spent and your start-up capital.

However, a business can only grow so big from its own income. In many cases, as a business grows, it gets to a point where the orders are so big that money must be borrowed to produce the product to fill them. With this kind of order, there is the risk that if the customer cannot pay or goes bankrupt, the business will also fail. At such a point, a business owner should investigate the credit-worthiness of the customer and weigh the risks. Some businesses have grown rapidly, some have gone under, and others have decided not to take the risk and stayed small. You can worry about that down the road.

# Using Your Savings

If you have savings you can tap to get your business started, that is the best source. You will not have to pay high interest rates, and you will not have to worry about paying anyone back.

*Home Equity*

If you have owned your home for several years, it is possible that the equity has grown substantially and you can get a second mortgage to finance your business. If you have been in the home for many years and have a good record of paying your bills, some lenders will make second mortgages that exceed the equity. Just remember, if your business fails, you may lose your house.

*Retirement Accounts*

Be careful about borrowing from your retirement savings. There are tax penalties for borrowing from or against certain types of retirement accounts. Also, your future financial security may be lost if your business does not succeed.

*Having Too Much Money*

It probably seems impossible to have too much money to start a business with, but many businesses have failed for that reason. With plenty of start-up capital available, a business owner does not need to watch expenses and can become wasteful. Employees get used to lavish spending. Once the money runs out and the business must run on its own earnings, it fails.

Starting with the bare minimum forces a business to watch its expenses and be frugal. It necessitates finding the least expensive solutions to problems that crop up and creative ways to be productive.

# Borrowing Money

It is extremely tempting to look to others to get the money to start a business. The risk of failure may be less worrisome and the pressure may be lower. However, there is a problem with borrowing. You may not have the same incentive to succeed if you are using someone else's money as you would if everything you own is on the line.

Actually, you should be even more concerned when using the money of others. Your reputation should be more valuable than the money itself, which can always be replaced. Yet, that is not always the case. How many people borrow again and again from their parents for failed business ventures?

*Family*  Depending on how much money your family can spare and the status of your relationship, borrowing from family members may be the most comfortable or most uncomfortable source of funds for you. If you have been assured a large inheritance and your parents have more funds than they need to live on, you may be able to borrow against your inheritance without worry. It will be your money anyway and you need it much more now than you will ten or more years from now. If you lose it all, it is your own loss anyway.

However, if you are borrowing your widowed mother's only source of income or asking her to cash in a CD she lives on to finance your get-rich-quick scheme, you should have second thoughts about it. Stop and consider all the real reasons your business might not take off and what your mother would do without the income.

*Friends*  Borrowing from friends is like borrowing from family members. If you know they have the funds available and could survive a loss, you may want to risk it. However, if they would be loaning you their only resources, do not chance it.

Financial problems can be the worst thing for a relationship, whether it is a casual friendship or a long term romantic involvement. Before you borrow from a friend, try to imagine what would happen if you could not pay it back and how you would feel if it caused the end of your relationship.

The ideal situation is if your friend were a co-venturer in your business, and the burden would not be totally on you to see how the funds were spent. Still, realize that such a venture will put extra strain on the relationship.

**Banks**    In a way, a bank can be a more comfortable party from which to borrow because you do not have a personal relationship with the bank as you do with a friend or family member. If you fail, they will write your loan off rather than disown you. However, a bank can also be the least comfortable party to borrow from because it will demand realistic projections and be on top of you to perform. If you do not meet the bank's expectations, it may call your loan just when you need it most.

The best thing about a bank loan is that they will require you to do your homework. You must have plans that make sense to a banker. If they approve your loan, you know that your plans are at least reasonable.

Bank loans are not cheap or easy. You will be paying a good interest rate, and you will have to put up collateral. If your business does not have equipment or receivables, the bank may require you to put up your house and other personal property to guarantee the loan.

Banks are a little easier to deal with when you get a *Small Business Administration* (SBA) loan. That is because the SBA guarantees that it will pay the bank if you default on the loan. SBA loans are obtained through local bank branches.

**Credit Cards**    Borrowing against a credit card is one of the fastest growing ways of financing a business, but it can be one of the most expensive ways, as the rates can go higher than twenty percent. However, there are many cards that offer lower rates and some people are able to get numerous cards. Some successful businesses have used the partners' credit cards to get off the ground or to weather through a cash crunch, but if the business does not begin to generate the cash to make the payments, you could soon end up in bankruptcy. A good strategy is only to use credit cards for a long term asset like a computer or for something that will quickly generate cash, like buying inventory to fill an order. Do not use credit cards to pay expenses that are not generating revenue.

# Getting a Rich Partner

One of the best business combinations is a young entrepreneur with ideas and ambition and a retired investor with business experience and money. Together, they can supply everything the business needs.

How to find such a partner? Be creative. You should have investigated the business you are starting and know others who have been in such businesses. Have any of them had partners retire over the last few years? Are any of them planning to phase out of the business?

# Selling Ownership Interests in Your Business

Silent investors are the best source of capital for your business. You retain full control of the business and if it happens to fail you have no obligation to them. Unfortunately, few silent investors are interested in a new business. It is only after you have proven your concept to be successful and built up a rather large enterprise that you will be able to attract such investors.

The most common way to obtain money from investors is to issue other types of stock or ownership interests to them. The best types of business entities for this are the corporation and the limited liability company. There is almost unlimited flexibility in the number and kinds of ownership interests you can issue.

If you do sell ownership interests in your business to outsiders, and even if you have co-owners that are involved in the business with you, you should make sure to have arrangements in place that govern what happens to those ownership interests if the owner dies, tries to voluntarily sell his or her interest, becomes disabled, or otherwise leaves the business. Disaster can strike when ownership interests pass to heirs or other transferees that you never contemplated having as business partners.

***Buy-Sell Agreements***
You can also protect yourself by providing yourself and your heirs with a way to *cash out* in the event that you die or become disabled. These arrangements are usually contained in a *buy-sell agreement*, in a corporation's *shareholders' agreement*, and in the *operating agreement* of a limited liability company. These agreements are complex and involve differing tax consequences. Consult an attorney to get the proper arrangements in place.

***Securities Laws***
There is one major problem with selling stock in your business and that is all of the federal and state regulations with which you must comply. Both the state and federal governments have long and complicated laws dealing with the sales of *securities*.

There are also hundreds of court cases attempting to explain what these laws mean. A thorough explanation of this area of law is beyond the scope of this book.

Basically, securities have been held to exist in any case in which a person provides money to someone with the expectation of getting a profit through the efforts of that person. This can apply to any situation in which someone buys stock or other ownership interest in, or makes a loan to, your business. What the laws require is disclosure of the risks involved and other material information that a person would use to decide whether to make the investment or not. In some cases, *registration* of the securities with the government is required. There are some *exemptions* to registration, such as for small amounts of money being raised and for limited numbers of investors.

Penalties for violation of securities laws are severe and include triple damages and prison terms. Consult a specialist in securities laws before issuing any security. You can often get an introductory consultation at a reasonable rate to learn your options.

# Using the Internet to Find Capital

In 1995, the owners of Wit Beer made headlines in all the business magazines by successfully raising $1.6 million for their business on the Internet. It seemed so easy, every business wanted to try. What was not made clear in most of the stories was that the owner was a corporate securities lawyer and that he did all of the necessary legal work to prepare a prospectus and properly register the stock, something that would have cost anyone else over $100,000 in legal fees. Also, most of the interest in the stock came from the articles, not from the Internet promotion. Today, a similar effort would probably not be nearly as successful.

Before attempting to market your company's shares on the Internet, be sure to get an opinion from a securities lawyer or do some serious research into securities laws.

The Internet does have some sources of capital listed. The following sites may be helpful.

**America's Business Funding Directory**
www.businessfinance.com

**Angel Capital Electronic Network**
http://acenet.csusb.edu

**Small Business Administration**
www.sba.gov

**FinanceHub**
www.financehub.com

**NVST**
www.nvst.com

*Inc.* **Magazine**
http://mothra.inc.com/finance

**The Capital Network**
www.thecapitalnetwork.com

# 5 | LOCATING YOUR BUSINESS

The right location for your business will be determined by what type of business it is and how fast you expect to grow. For some types of businesses, the location will not be important to your success or failure. In others, it will be crucial.

## Working Out of Your Home

Many small businesses get started out of the home. Chapter 6 discusses the *legalities* of home businesses. This section discusses the *practicalities*.

Starting a business out of your home can save you the rent, electricity, insurance, and other costs of setting up at another location. For some people this is ideal and they can combine their home and work duties easily and efficiently. For others, it is a disaster. A spouse, children, neighbors, television, and household chores can be so distracting that no other work gets done.

***Phone Lines***      You also should consider whether the type of business you are starting is compatible with a home office. For example, if your business mostly consists of making phone calls or calling clients, the home may be an ideal place to run it.

The home may not be a good location if your clients need to visit you or you will need daily pickups and deliveries by truck. This is discussed in more detail in the next chapter.

Since residential rates are usually lower than business lines, many people use their residential telephone line to conduct business or add a second residential line. However, if you wish to be listed in the Yellow Pages, you will need to have a business line in your home. If you are running two or more types of businesses, you can probably add their names as additional listings on the original number and avoid paying for another business line.

# Choosing a Retail Site

For most types of retail stores, the location is of prime importance. Such things to consider are how close it is to your potential customers, how visible it is to the public, and how easily accessible it is to both autos and pedestrians. The attractiveness and safety should also be considered.

Location would be less important for a business that was the only one of its kind in the area. For example, if there was only one moped parts dealer or Armenian restaurant in a metropolitan area, people would have to come to wherever you are if they want your products or services. However, even with such businesses, keep in mind that there is competition. People who want moped parts can order them by mail and restaurant customers can choose another type of cuisine.

You should look up all the businesses like the one you plan online or in the phone book and mark them on a map. For some businesses, like a cleaners, you would want to be far from the others. But for other businesses, like antique stores, you would want to be near the others. (Antique stores usually do not carry the same things, they do not compete, and people like to go to an *antique district* and visit all the shops.)

# Choosing an Office, Manufacturing, or Warehouse Space

If your business will be the type in which customers will not come to you, such as a manufacturing operation or warehouse facility, locating it near customers is not as much of a concern. You can probably save money by locating away from the high traffic, central business districts. However, you should consider the convenience for employees and not locate in an area that would be unattractive to them or too far from where they would likely live.

For manufacturing or warehouse operations, you should consider your proximity to a post office, trucking company, or rail line. Where several sites are available, you might consider which one has the earliest or most convenient pick-up schedule for the carriers you plan to use.

# Leasing a Site

A lease of space can be one of the biggest expenses of a small business, so you should do a lot of homework before signing one. There are a lot of terms in a commercial lease that can make or break your business. The following are the most critical.

**Zoning**    Before signing a lease, you should be sure that everything that your business will need to do is allowed by the zoning of the property.

**Restrictions**    In some shopping centers, existing tenants have guarantees that other tenants do not compete with them. For example, if you plan to open a restaurant and bakery, you may be forbidden to sell carry-out baked goods if the supermarket has a bakery and a noncompete clause.

**Signs**    Business signs are regulated by zoning laws, sign laws, and property restrictions. If you rent a hidden location with no possibility for adequate signage, your business will have a lot smaller chance of success than with a more visible site or much larger sign.

**ADA Compliance**    The *Americans with Disabilities Act* (ADA) requires that reasonable accommodations be made to make businesses accessible to the handicapped. When a business is remodeled, many more changes are required than if no remodeling is done. When renting space, you should be sure that it complies with the law, that the landlord will be responsible for compliance, or that you are aware of the full costs you will bear.

**Expansion**

As your business grows, you may need to expand your space. The time to find out about your options is before you sign the lease. Perhaps you you can take over adjoining units when those leases expire.

**Renewal**

Location is a key to success for some businesses. If you spend five years building up a clientele, you do not want someone to take over your locale at the end of your lease. Therefore, you should have a renewal clause on your lease. This usually allows an increase in rent based on inflation.

**Guaranty**

Most landlords of commercial space will not rent to a small corporation without a personal guaranty of the lease. This is a very risky thing for a new business owner to do. The lifetime rent on a long-term commercial lease can be hundreds of thousands of dollars. If your business fails, the last thing you want to do is be personally responsible for several years of rent.

Where space is scarce or a location is hot, a landlord can get the guarantees he or she demands and there is nothing you can do about it (except perhaps set up an asset protection plan ahead of time). But when several units are vacant or the commercial rental market is soft, you can often negotiate out of the personal guaranty. If the lease is five years, maybe you can get away with a guaranty of just the first year. Give it a try.

**Duty to Open**

Some shopping centers have rules requiring all shops to be open certain hours. If you cannot afford to staff it the whole time required or if you have religious or other reasons that make this a problem, you should negotiate it out of the lease or find another location.

**Sublease**

At some point you may decide to sell your business. In many cases, your business' location is the most valuable aspect of it. For this reason you should be sure that you have the right to either *assign* your lease or to *sublease* the property.

If this is impossible, one way around a prohibition is to incorporate your business before signing the lease and then when you sell the business, sell the stock. But some lease clauses prohibit transfer of *any interest* in the business, so read the lease carefully.

# Buying a Site

If you are experienced with owning rental property, you will probably be more inclined to buy a site for your business. If you have no experience with real estate, you should probably rent and not take on the extra cost and responsibility of property ownership.

One reason to buy your site is that you can build up equity. Rather than pay rent to a landlord you can pay off a mortgage and eventually own the property.

**Separating the Ownership**

One risk in buying a business site is that if the business gets into financial trouble the creditors may go after the building as well. For this reason, most people who buy a site for their business keep the ownership out of the business. For example, the business will be a corporation and the real estate will be owned personally by the owner or by a trust unrelated to the business.

**Expansion**

Before buying a site, you should consider the growth potential of your business. If it grows quickly, will you be able to expand at that site or will you have to move? Might the property next door be available for sale in the future if you need it? Can you get an option on it?

If the site is a good investment, whether or not your business is located on it, then by all means buy it. But if its main use is for your business, think twice.

**Zoning**

When you buy a site, you might be faced with the some of the same concerns you would have if you were renting. You will want to make sure that the zoning permits the type of business you wish to start or that you can get a variance without a large expense or delay. Be aware that just because a business is now using the site does not mean that you can expand or remodel the business at that site. Some zoning laws allow businesses to be grandfathered in, but not expanded. Check with the zoning department and find out exactly what is allowed.

**Signs**

Signs are another concern. Some cities have regulated signs and do not allow new or larger ones. Some businesses have used these laws to get publicity. A car dealer who was told to take down a large number of American flags on his lot filed a federal lawsuit and rallied the community behind him.

**ADA Compliance**
ADA compliance is another concern when buying a commercial building. Find out from the building department if the building is in compliance or what needs to be done to put it in compliance. If you remodel, the requirements may be more strict.

NOTE: *When dealing with public officials, keep in mind that they do not always know what the law is or do not accurately explain it. They often try to intimidate people into doing things that are not required by law. Read the requirements yourself and question the officials if they seem to be interpreting it wrong. Seek legal advice if officials refuse to reexamine the law or move away from an erroneous position.*

NOTE: *Also consider that keeping public officials happy may be worth the price. If you are already doing something they have overlooked, do not make a big deal over a little thing they want changed, or they may subject you to a full inspection or audit.*

# Check Governmental Regulations

When looking for a site for your business, you should investigate the different government regulations in your area. For example, a location just outside the city or county limits might have a lower licensing fee, a lower sales tax rate, and less strict signage requirements.

# 6 LICENSING YOUR BUSINESS

Some Massachusetts cities require you to obtain an occupational license. If you are in a city, you may need both a city and a state license. Businesses that do work in several cities sometimes must obtain a license from each city in which they do work.

City licenses are usually available at city hall. Be sure to find out if zoning allows your type of business before buying or leasing property. The licensing departments will check the zoning before issuing your license.

If you will be preparing or serving food, you will need to check with the local health department to be sure that the premises are in compliance with their regulations.

## Home Businesses

Problems occasionally arise when persons attempt to start a business in their home. Small new businesses cannot afford to pay rent for commercial space and cities often try to forbid business in residential areas. Getting an occupational license or advertising a fictitious name often gives notice to the city that a business is being conducted in a residential area.

Some people avoid the problem by starting their businesses without obtaining the necessary licenses or fictitious name filings, figuring that the penalties for not having done so (if they are caught) are less expensive than the cost of office space. Some also avoid zoning restrictions. If a person regularly parks commercial trucks and equipment on his or her property, has delivery trucks coming and going, or employee cars parked along the street, there will probably be complaints from neighbors and the city will probably take legal action. But if a person's business consists merely of making phone calls out of the home and keeping supplies there, the problem may never become an issue.

If a problem does arise regarding a home business that does not disturb the neighbors, a good argument can be made that the zoning law that prohibits the business is unconstitutional. When zoning laws were first instituted, they were not meant to stop people from doing things in a residence that had historically been part of the life in a residence. Consider an artist. Should a zoning law prohibit a person from sitting in his home and painting pictures? If he sells them for a living is there a difference? Should the government be able to force him to rent commercial space just because he decides to sell the paintings he paints?

Similar arguments can be made for many home businesses. For hundreds of years people performed income-producing activities in their homes. (The authors are waiting for their city fathers to tell them to stop writing books in their home offices.) But court battles with a city are expensive and probably not worth the effort for a small business. The best course of action is to keep a low profile. Using a post office box for the business is sometimes helpful in diverting attention away from the residence.

# State Regulated Professions

The state requires licensing of certain professions and occupations. If you are in a regulated profession, you should be aware of the laws that apply to your profession. The following pages contain a list of many of these professions and the state laws covering them. You can make copies of these laws and related regulations at any law library. You can also find these laws on the Internet at **www.state.ma.us./legis/laws/mgl/index.htm**.

If you do not think your profession is regulated, you should read through the list anyway. Some of those included may surprise you.

### Regulated Professions in Massachusetts
### and the Statutes Governing Them
*Citations are to Massachusetts General Laws (M.G.L.)*

(If no Sections are specified, the entire chapter cited applies.)

| Profession | M.G.L. Chapter | Section(s) |
|---|---|---|
| Auctioneers | 100 | |
| Physicians and Surgeons | 112 | 2-9B |
| Physicians Assistants | 112 | 9C-9K |
| Podiatrists | 112 | 13-22 |
| Athletic Trainers and Occupational/Physical Therapists | 112 | 23A-23Q |
| Respiratory Therapists | 112 | 23R-23BB |
| Pharmacists | 112 | 24-36 |
| Sellers of Drugs | 112 | 36A-42A |
| Dentists | 112 | 43-53 |
| Veterinarians | 112 | 54-60 |
| Architects | 112 | 60A-60O |
| Optometrists | 112 | 66-73B |
| Dispensing Opticians | 112 | 73C-73M |
| Nurses | 112 | 74-81C |
| Professional Engineers and Land Surveyors | 112 | 81D-81T |

| | | |
|---|---|---|
| Embalmers and Funeral Directors | 112 | 82-87 |
| Certified Public Accountants | 112 | 87A-87E 1/2 |
| Barbers | 112 | 87F-87S |
| Cosmetologists | 112 | 87T-87KK |
| Sanitarians | 112 | 87LL-87OO |
| Real Estate Brokers and Salesmen | 112 | 87PP-87DDD 1/2 |
| Electrologists | 112 | 87EEE-87OOO |
| Radio and Television Technicians | 112 | 87PPP-87VVV |
| Certified Health Officers | 112 | 87WWW-87ZZZ |
| Drinking Water Supply Facility Operators | 112 | 87CCCC-87DDDD |
| Chiropractors | 112 | 89-97 |
| Landscape Architects | 112 | 98-107 |
| Nursing Home Administrators | 112 | 108-117 |
| Psychologists | 112 | 118-129A |
| Social Workers | 112 | 130-137 |
| Speech-Language Pathologists and Audiologists | 112 | 138-147 |
| Acupuncturists | 112 | 148-162 |
| Allied Mental Health and Human Services Professionals | 112 | 163-172 |
| Real Estate Appraisers | 112 | 173-195 |

| | | |
|---|---|---|
| Labeling, Distribution, Sale, Storage, Transportation, Use and Disposal of Pesticides | 132B | |
| Attorneys | 221 | 37-52 |
| Financing Motor Vehicles | 255B | |
| Certain Mortgage Brokers and Lenders | 255E | |

# Federal Licenses

So far, there are few businesses that require federal registration. If you are in any of the types of businesses listed, check with the federal agency that regulates the business.

Radio or television stations or manufacturers of equipment emitting radio waves:

**Federal Communications Commission**
445 12th Street SW
Washington, DC 20554
www.fcc.gov

Manufacturers of alcohol, tobacco or firearms:

**Bureau of Alcohol, Tobacco and Firearms**
Office of Public and Governmental Affairs
650 Massachusetts Avenue, NW
Room 8290
Washington, DC 20226
www.atf.treas.gov

Securities brokers and providers of investment advice:

**SEC**
450 Fifth Street, NW
Washington, DC 20549
www.sec.gov

Manufacturers of drugs and processors of meat:

**Food and Drug Administration**
5600 Fishers Lane
Rockville, MD 20857
www.fda.gov

Interstate carriers:

**Surface Transportation Board**
1925 K Street, NW
Washington, DC 20423
www.stb.dot.gov

Exporting:

**Bureau of Export Administration**
Department of Commerce
14th Street & Constitution Avenue, NW
Washington, DC 20220
www.bxa.doc.gov

| 7 | CONTRACT LAWS |
|---|---|

As a business owner, you will need to know the basics of forming a simple contract for your transactions with both customers and vendors. There is a lot of misunderstanding about what the law is and people may give you erroneous information. Relying on it can cost you money. This chapter gives you a quick overview of the principles that apply to your transactions and the pitfalls to avoid. If you face more complicated contract questions, consult a law library or an attorney familiar with small business law.

## Traditional Contract Law

One of the first things taught in law school is that a *contract* is not legal unless three elements are present: offer, acceptance, and consideration. During the rest of the semester in contracts class, the students dissect exactly what may be a valid offer, acceptance, and consideration. For your purposes, the important things to remember include the following.

- ✪ If you make an *offer* to someone, it may result in a binding contract, even if you change your mind or find out it was a bad deal for you.

- ✪ Unless an offer is *accepted* and both parties agree to the same terms, there is no contract.

✪ A contract does not always have to be in *writing*. Some laws require certain contracts to be in writing, but as a general rule an oral contract is legal. (The problem is proving that the contract existed.)

✪ Without *consideration* (the exchange of something of value or mutual promises), there is not a valid contract.

As mentioned, an entire semester is spent analyzing each of the three elements of a contract. The most important rules for the business owner are as follows.

✪ *An advertisement is not an offer.* Suppose you put an ad in the newspaper offering *New IBM computers only $1995!* but there is a typo in the ad and it says $19.95? Can people come in and say *I accept, here's my $19.95*, thereby creating a legal contract? Fortunately, no. Courts have ruled that the ad is not an offer that a person can accept. It is an *invitation* to come in and make offers, which the business can accept or reject.

✪ *The same rule applies to the price tag on an item.* If someone switches price tags on your merchandise or if you accidentally put the wrong price on it, you are not required by law to sell it at that price. If you intentionally put the wrong price, you may be liable under *bait and switch* laws. Many merchants honor a mistaken price just because refusing to would constitute bad will and probably lose a customer.

✪ *When a person makes an offer, several things may happen.* It may be *accepted*, creating a legal contract. It may be *rejected*. It may *expire* before it has been accepted, or it may be *withdrawn* before acceptance. A contract may expire either by a date made in the offer (*e.g., This offer remains open until noon on January 29, 2005*) or after a reasonable amount of time. What is reasonable is a legal question which a court must decide. If someone makes you an offer to sell goods, clearly you cannot come back five years later and accept. Can you accept a week later or a month later and create a legal contract? That depends on the type of goods and the circumstances.

✪ *A person accepting an offer cannot add any terms to it.* If you offer to sell a car for $1,000 and the other party says they accept as long as you put new tires on it, there is no contract. An acceptance with changed terms is considered a rejection and a counteroffer.

✪ When someone rejects your offer and makes a counteroffer, *a contract can be created by your acceptance of the counteroffer.*

These rules can affect your business on a daily basis. Suppose you offer to sell something to one customer over the phone and five minutes later another customer walks in and offers you more for it. To protect yourself, you should call the first customer and withdraw your offer before accepting the offer of the second customer. If the first customer accepts before you have withdrawn your offer, you may be sued if you have sold the item to the second customer.

**Exceptions**     There are a few exceptions to the basic rules of contracts. These exceptions include the following.

✪     *Consent to a contract must be voluntary.* If it is made under a threat, the contract is not valid. If a business refuses to give a person's car back unless they pay $200 for changing the oil, the customer could probably sue and get the $200 back.

✪     *Contracts to do illegal acts or acts against public policy are not enforceable.* If an electrician signs a contract to put some illegal wiring in a house, the customer could probably not force the electrician to do it because the court would refuse to require an illegal act.

✪     *If either party to an offer dies, the offer expires and cannot be accepted by the heirs.* If a painter is hired to paint a portrait and dies before completing it, his wife cannot finish it and require payment. However, a corporation does not die, even if its owners die. If a corporation is hired to build a house and the corporation's owner dies, that person's heirs may take over the corporation and finish the job and require payment.

✪     *Contracts made under misrepresentation are not enforceable.* For example, if someone tells you a car has thirty-five thousand miles on it, you agree to buy it, and you later discover it has one hundred thirty-five thousand miles, you may be able to rescind the contract for fraud and misrepresentation.

✪     *If there were a mutual mistake a contract may be rescinded.* For example, if both you and the seller thought the car had thirty-five thousand miles on it and both relied on that assumption, the contract could be rescinded. However, if the seller knew the car has one hundred thirty-five thousand miles on it, but you assumed it had thirty-five thousand and did not ask, you probably could not rescind the contract.

# Statutory Contract Law

The previous section discussed the basics of contract law. These basics are not usually stated in a state's statutes, but are the legal principles decided by judges over hundreds of years. The legislatures in recent times have made numerous exceptions to these principles. In most cases, these laws have been passed when the legislature felt that traditional law was not fair. The important laws that affect contracts are the following.

**Statutes of Fraud**

The *statutes of fraud* state when a contract must be in writing to be valid. Some people believe a contract is not valid unless it is in writing, but that is not so. Only those types of contracts mentioned in the statutes of fraud must be in writing. Of course, an oral contract is much harder to prove in court than one that is in writing.

In Massachusetts, some of the contracts that must be in writing, and the applicable statute sections, are as follows:

- ✪ sales of any interest in real estate (Mass. Gen. Laws, ch. 259, Sec. 1);

- ✪ guarantees of debts of another person (Mass. Gen. Laws, ch. 259, Sec. 1);

- ✪ agreements which take more than one year to complete (Mass. Gen. Laws, ch. 259, Sec. 1);

- ✪ promises by executors, administrators, or assignees in insolvency to pay damages from their own estates (Mass. Gen. Laws, ch. 259, Sec. 1);

- ✪ prenuptial agreements (Mass. Gen. Laws, ch. 259, Sec. 1);

- ✪ agreements concerning making or revoking a will or codicil or making a devise (Mass. Gen. Laws, ch. 259, Sec. 5, 5A);

- ✪ sales of goods over $500 (Mass. Gen. Laws, ch. 106, Sec. 2-201); and,

- ✪ sales of personal property of over $5,000 (Mass. Gen. Laws, ch. 106, Sec. 1-206).

**Consumer Protection Law**

Because of alleged unfair practices by some types of businesses, laws have been passed controlling transactions between consumers and certain businesses. Most notable among these are agreements arising from door-to-door solicitations. These agreements would cover:

> *the sale or lease of goods or the rendering of services, or both, primarily for personal, family, or household purposes of over $25 and which are consummated at a place other than the address of the seller or lessor.*

These types of agreements may be canceled within three business days. Retail installment sales contracts may also be cancelled within three business days. Motor vehicle retail installment sales contracts may be canceled under certain circumstances. These laws are described in more detail in the section on *Advertising Laws and Rules* in Chapter 11.

# Preparing Your Contracts

Before you open your business, you should obtain or prepare the contracts or policies you will use in it. In some businesses, such as a restaurant, you may not need much. Perhaps you will want a sign near the entrance stating *shirt and shoes required* or *diners must be seated by 10:30 P.M.*

However, if you are a building contractor or run a similar business, you will need detailed contracts to use with your customers. If you do not clearly spell out your rights and obligations, you may end up in court and lose thousands of dollars in profits.

Of course, the best way to have an effective contract is to have an attorney, who is experienced in the subject, prepare one to meet the needs of your business. However, since this may be too expensive for your new operation, you may want to go elsewhere. Three sources for the contracts you will need are other business like yours, trade associations, and legal form books. You should obtain as many different contracts as possible, compare them, and decide which terms are most comfortable for you.

# 8 | INSURANCE

There are not many laws requiring you to have insurance, but if you do not have insurance you may face liability that could ruin your business. You should be aware of the types insurance available, and weigh the risks of a loss against the cost of policy.

Be aware that there can be a wide range of prices and coverage in insurance policies. Get at least three quotes from different insurance agents and ask each one to explain the benefits of his or her policy.

## Workers' Compensation

In general, if you have any employees, you are required by law to carry *workers' compensation insurance*.

The term *employee* is specifically defined in Massachusetts General Laws, Chapter 152. You should read this law carefully if you think you need to comply with this law. For example, part-time employees, students, aliens, and illegal workers count as employees. However, under certain conditions, professional athletes, real estate agents, part-time domestic workers, seamen, taxi cab drivers, casual and seasonal workers, and door-to-door salespeople are not considered employees. Independent contractors are also not considered employees.

Even if you are not required to have workers' compensation insurance, you may still wish to carry it because it can protect you from litigation.

This insurance can be obtained from most insurance companies and, in many cases, is not expensive. If you have such coverage, you are protected against suits by employees or their heirs in case of an accident.

Failure to provide workers' compensation insurance when required is considered serious. It could result in a substantial fine, prison time, and an injunction against employing anyone. If a person is injured on a job, even if another employee caused it or the injured person contributed to his or her own injury, you may be required to pay for all resulting losses.

There are reporting requirements under workers' compensation law, so make sure you read and understand what your policy requires. Also, it is a misdemeanor to deduct the amount of the premiums from the employee's wages.

# Unemployment Insurance

Massachusetts requires employers who employ one or more permanent, temporary, or part-time workers to provide information to the Department of Employment and Training (D.E.T.) regarding its employees. The D.E.T. will determine whether the employer must make unemployment insurance contributions. A sample **EMPLOYER STATUS REPORT** that provides this information is in Appendix A at page 185. A blank **EMPLOYER STATUS REPORT** is contained in Appendix B. (see form 10, p.219.)

The unemployment insurance system is a state system, administered by the Department of Employment and Training. Employers who fail to pay required contributions are subject to various civil and criminal penalties, which include up to $50,000 and five years in jail for certain infractions.

# Liability Insurance

Liability insurance can be divided into two main areas: coverage for injuries on your premises and by your employees; and coverage for injuries caused by your products.

Coverage for the first type of injury is usually very reasonably priced. Injuries in your business or by your employees (such as in an auto accident) are covered by standard premises or auto policies. But coverage for injuries by products may be harder to find and more expensive. In the current liability crisis, juries have awarded high judgments for accidents involving products that had little if any impact on the accident. The situation has become so bad that some entire industries have gone out of business or moved overseas.

***Asset Protection*** The best way to find out if insurance is available for your type of business is to check with other businesses. If there is a trade group for your industry, their newsletter or magazine may contain ads for insurers. If insurance is unavailable or unaffordable, you can go without and use a corporation and other asset protection devices to protect yourself from liability.

***Umbrella Policy*** As a business owner, you will be a more visible target for lawsuits even if there is little merit to them. Lawyers know that a *nuisance suit* is often settled for thousands of dollars. Because of your greater exposure, consider getting a personal *umbrella policy*. This is a policy that covers you for claims of up to one, two, or even five million dollars and is very reasonably priced.

# Hazard Insurance

One of the worst things that can happen to your business is a fire, flood, or other disaster. With lost customer lists, inventory, and equipment, many businesses have been forced to close after such a disaster.

The premium for such insurance is usually reasonable and could protect you from loss of your business. You can even get business interruption insurance that will cover your losses while your business is getting back on its feet.

# Home Business Insurance

There is a special insurance problem for home businesses. Most homeowner and tenant insurance policies do not cover business activities. In fact, under some policies you may be denied coverage if you used your home for a business.

If you merely use your home to make business phone calls and send letters, you will probably not have a problem and not need extra coverage. But if you own equipment, or have dedicated a portion of your home exclusively to the business, you could have a problem. Check with your insurance agent for the options that are available to you.

If your business is a sole proprietorship, and you have, say, a computer that you use both personally and for your business, it would probably be covered under your homeowners' policy. But if you incorporate your business and bought the computer in the name of the corporation, coverage might be denied. If a computer is your main business asset you could get a special insurance policy in the company name covering just the computer. One company that offers such a policy is Safeware at 800-723-9273 or 800-800-1492.

# Automobile Insurance

If you or any of your employees will be using an automobile for business purposes, be sure that such use is covered. Sometimes a policy may include an exclusion for business use. Check to be sure your liability policy covers you if one of your employees causes an accident while running a business errand.

# Health Insurance

While new businesses can rarely afford health insurance for their employees, the sooner they can obtain it, the better chance they will have to find and keep good employees. Those starting a business usually need insurance for themselves (unless they have a working spouse who can cover the family) and they can sometimes get a better rate if they get a small business package. Many local chambers of commerce offer group health insurance plans to small businesses.

# Employee Theft

If you fear employees may be able to steal from your business, you may want to have them *bonded*. This means that you pay an insurance company a premium to guarantee employees' honesty, and if they cheat you the insurance company pays you damages. This can cover all existing and new employees.

# 9 HEALTH AND SAFETY LAWS

There are federal and state laws that relate to the health and safety of workers and customers. As a business owner you are liable under these laws and need to comply with them.

## OSHA

The *Occupational Safety and Health Administration* (OSHA) is a good example of government regulation so severe it can strangle businesses out of existence. The point of the law is to place the duty on the employer to keep the workplace free from recognized hazards that are likely to cause death or serious bodily injury to workers.

If you have ten or fewer employees or if you are in certain types of businesses, you do not have to keep a record of employees' illnesses, injuries, and exposure to hazardous substances. If you have eleven or more employees, you do have to keep this record, which is called *Log 200*. All employers are required to display a poster that you can get from OSHA.

Within forty-eight hours of an on-the-job death of an employee or injury of five or more employees on the job, the area director of OSHA must be contacted.

For more information, you should write or call an OSHA office:

**U.S. Department of Labor**
200 Constitution Avenue, NW
Room N-3101
Washington, DC 20210
Boston: 617-565-9860

You can also visit their website at **www.osha-slc.gov** and obtain copies of their publications, *OSHA Handbook for Small Business* (OSHA 2209) and *OSHA Publications and Audiovisual Programs Catalog* (OSHA 2019). They also have a poster that is required to be posted in the workplace at **www.osha.gov/oshpubs/poster.html**.

*Hazard Communication Standard*

The Hazard Communication Standard requires that employees be made aware of the hazards in the workplace. (Title 29, Code of Federal Regulations (C.F.R.), Section (Sec.) 1910.1200.) It is especially applicable to those working with chemicals but this can include even offices that use copy machines. Businesses using hazardous chemicals must have a comprehensive program for informing employees of the hazards and for protecting them from contamination.

For more information, you can contact OSHA at the previously-mentioned addresses, phone numbers, or websites. They can supply a copy of the regulation and a booklet called *OSHA 3084*, which explains the law.

# EPA

The Worker Protection Standard for Agricultural Pesticides requires safety training, decontamination sites and, of course, posters. The *Environmental Protection Agency* will provide information on compliance with this law. They can be reached at 800-490-9198 or their website at **www.epa.gov**. They can also be reached by mail at: the following address.

**Environmental Protection Agency**
1200 Pennsylvania Avenue, NW
Washington, DC 20460

# FDA

The *Pure Food and Drug Act of 1906* prohibits the misbranding or adulteration of food and drugs. It also created the *Food and Drug Administration* (FDA), has promulgated tons of regulations and must give permission before a new drug can be introduced into the market. If you will be dealing with any food or drugs you should keep abreast of their policies. Their website is **www.fda.gov**, their small business site is **www.fda.gov/ora/fed_state/small_business** and their local small business representative is:

> **FDA, Northeast Region**
> Small Business Representative
> 158-15 Liberty Avenue
> Jamaica, NY 11433-1034
> 718-662-5618

# Hazardous Material Transportation

There are regulations that control the shipping and packing of hazardous materials. For more information contact:

> **Office of Hazardous Materials Safety**
> Research and Special Programs Administration
> U.S. Department of Transportation
> 400 7th Street, SW
> Washington, DC 20590
> 202-366-8553

For an organizational structure and phone contacts, visit **http://hazmat.dot.gov/org&ct.htm**.

# CPSC

The Consumer Product Safety Commission (CPSC) has a set of rules that cover the safety of products. The commission feels that because its rules cover products, rather than people or companies, they apply to everyone producing such products. However, federal laws do not apply to small businesses that do not affect interstate commerce. Whether a small business would fall under a CPSC rule would depend on the size and nature of the business.

The CPSC rules are contained in The Code of Federal Regulations, Title 16 in the following parts. These can be found at most law libraries, some public libraries, and on the Internet at **www.access.gpo.gov/nara/cfr/cfr-table-search.html**. The CPSC's site is at **http://cpsc.gov/index.html**.

| Product | Part |
|---|---|
| Antennas, CB and TV | 1402 |
| Architectural Glazing Material | 1201 |
| Articles Hazardous to Children Under 3 | 1501 |
| Baby Cribs-Full Size | 1508 |
| Baby Cribs-Non-Full Size | 1509 |
| Bicycle Helmets | 1203 |
| Bicycles | 1512 |
| Carpets and Rugs | 1630, 1631 |
| Cellulose Insulation | 1209, 1404 |
| Cigarette Lighters | 1210 |
| Citizens Band Base Station Antennas | 1204 |
| Coal and Wood Burning Appliances | 1406 |
| Consumer Products Containing Chlorofluorocarbons | 1401 |
| Electrically Operated Toys | 1505 |
| Emberizing Materials Containing Asbestos (banned) | 1305 |
| Extremely Flammable Contact Adhesives (banned) | 1302 |
| Fireworks | 1507 |
| Garage Door Openers | 1211 |
| Hazardous Lawn Darts (banned) | 1306 |
| Hazardous Substances | 1500 |
| Human Subjects | 1028 |
| Lawn Mowers, Walk-Behind | 1205 |
| Lead-Containing Paint (banned) | 1303 |
| Matchbooks | 1202 |
| Mattresses | 1632 |
| Pacifiers | 1511 |
| Patching Compounds Containing Asbestos (banned) | 1304 |
| Poisons | 1700 |
| Rattles | 1510 |
| Self-Pressurized Consumer Products | 1401 |
| Sleepwear-Children's | 1615, 1616 |
| Swimming Pool Slides | 1207 |
| Toys, Electrical | 1505 |
| Unstable Refuse Bins (banned) | 1301 |

# Additional Regulations

There are proposals for new laws and regulations every day. It would be impossible to include every conceivable one in this book. To be up to date on the laws that affect your type of business, you should belong to a trade association for your industry and subscribe to newsletters that cover your industry. Attending industry conventions is a good way to learn more and to discover new ways to increase your profits.

# Smoking

Massachusetts has laws that prohibit smoking in the following places:

- ✪ public elevators;

- ✪ supermarkets and retail food outlets;

- ✪ in or upon any public mass transit conveyances or indoor platform or enclosed outdoor platform;

- ✪ at any open meeting of a government body;

- ✪ any courtroom;

- ✪ the State House;

- ✪ any building owned by the Commonwealth; and,

- ✪ any space occupied by a state agency or department of the Commonwealth.

No one may smoke in any of the following places except in specifically designated smoking areas:

- ✪ courthouse
- ✪ school
- ✪ college
- ✪ university
- ✪ museum
- ✪ library
- ✪ train
- ✪ airplane

- ✪ waiting area of an airport
- ✪ waiting area of a health care facility
- ✪ group child care center
- ✪ school-aged day care center
- ✪ family day care center
- ✪ any public building
- ✪ any restaurant with a seating capacity of seventy-five or more persons

Areas within the listed locations can be designated as a smoking area only if nonsmoking areas of sufficient size and capacity are available to accommodate nonsmokers. Any person admitted to a health-care facility must, upon request, be assigned a room in which smoking is not permitted. Notices must be placed at entrances to describe the above smoking prohibitions and to designate smoking areas and nonsmoking areas.

The law allows smoking in a completely enclosed private office used by an individual within any of the listed facilities, public buildings, vehicles, or places except the State House, any building owned by the Commonwealth, and any space occupied by a state agency or department of the Commonwealth (not including state hospitals and substance abuse treatment centers).

# 10 EMPLOYMENT AND LABOR LAWS

For small businesses, there are not many rules regarding whom you may hire or fire. Fortunately, the ancient law that an employee can be fired at any time (or may quit at any time) still prevails for small businesses. But in certain situations, and as you grow, you will come under a number of laws that affect your hiring and firing practices.

## Hiring Laws

One of the most important things to consider when hiring someone is that if you fire them, they may be entitled to unemployment compensation. If so, your unemployment insurance contributions will likely go up and it can cost you a lot of money. Therefore, only hire people whom you are sure you will keep and avoid situations in which your former employees can collect unemployment.

One way this can be done is by hiring only part-time employees. The drawback to this is that you may not be able to attract the best employees. When hiring dishwashers or busboys, this may not be an issue, but when hiring someone to develop a software product, you do not want them to leave halfway through the development.

A better solution is to screen applicants and only hire those who you feel certain will succeed. Of course, this is easier said than done. Some people interview well but then turn out to be incompetent at the job.

The best record to look for is someone who has stayed a long time at each of their previous jobs. Next best is someone who has not stayed as long (for good reasons) but has always been employed. The worst type of hire would be someone who is or has been collecting unemployment compensation.

In the authors' experience, the intelligence of an employee is more important than his or her experience. An employee with years of typing experience may be fast but unable to figure out how to use your new computer. On the other hand, an intelligent employee can learn the equipment quickly and eventually gain speed. Of course, common sense is important in all situations.

The bottom line is that you cannot know if an employee will be able to fill your needs from a resumé and interview. Once you have found someone who you think will work out, offer him or her a job with a ninety day probationary period. If you are not completely satisfied with him or her after the ninety days, offer to extend the probationary period for ninety additional days rather than end the relationship immediately. Of course, all of this should be in writing.

**Background Checks**

Checking references is important, but beware that a former boss may be a good friend or even a relative. Some may consider it acceptable to exaggerate on resumés, but in recent years, some applicants have been found to be completely fabricating sections of their education and experience.

**Polygraph Tests**

Under the federal *Employee Polygraph Protection Act*, you cannot require an employee or prospective employee to take a polygraph test unless you are in the armored car, guard, or pharmaceutical business. Under Massachusetts law, employers may not use lie detector tests on any employee or applicant for employment. Applications must contain a written notice stating that lie detector testing is illegal.

**Medical Examinations**

Employers may conduct medical exams, at the employer's expense, only for the purpose of determining whether the employee is capable of performing the job with reasonable accommodation. Employers may not require AIDS/HIV testing as a condition of employment. Upon request, a copy of the medical report must be furnished to the employee.

***Drug Tests***   Under the ADA, drug testing can only be required of applicants who have been offered jobs conditioned upon passing the drug test. Massachusetts does not have a statute limiting or prohibiting drug testing, but drug tests would be susceptible to challenges under broad statutes such as privacy laws.

# New Hire Reporting

A federal law was passed in 1996 that requires the reporting of new hires. This is the *Personal Responsibility and Work Opportunity Reconciliation Act of 1996* (PRWORA). It provides that such information must be reported by employers to their state government. Massachusetts has had a similar law since 1993.

Massachusetts law requires that within fourteen days of hiring a new employee, an employer must provide the state with information about the employee including his or her name, Social Security number, and address. This information can be submitted in several ways including mail, fax, magnetic tape, or over the Internet. There is a special form that can be used for this reporting; however, an employer can use the **IRS Form W-4** (form 7, p.213) for this purpose. Since this form must be filled out for all employees anyway, it would be pointless to use a separate form for the new hire reporting. A copy of **IRS Form W-4** may be faxed to 617-887-5049 or mailed to:

**Department of Revenue**
P.O. Box 7032
Boston, MA 02204

You can call them at 800-332-2733 or visit their website at **www.dor.state.ma.us** for more information about the program.

# Employment Agreements

To avoid misunderstanding with employees, you should use an employment agreement or an employee handbook. These can spell out in detail the policies of your company and the rights of your employees. They can protect your trade secrets and spell out clearly that employment can be terminated at any time by either party.

While it may be difficult or awkward to ask an existing employee to sign such an agreement, an applicant hoping you will hire them will usually sign whatever is necessary to obtain the job. However, because of the unequal bargaining position, you should not use an agreement that would make you look bad if the matter ever went to court.

If having an employee sign an agreement is awkward, you can usually obtain the same rights by putting the company policies in an employee manual. Each existing and new employee should be given a copy of the manual, along with a letter stating that the rules apply to all employees and that by accepting or continuing employment at your company they agree to abide by the rules. Having an employee sign a receipt for the letter and manual is proof that they received it.

One danger of an employment agreement or handbook is that it may be interpreted to create a long-term employment contract. To avoid this, be sure that you clearly state in the agreement or handbook that the employment is *at will* and can be terminated at any time by either party for any or no reason.

Some other things to consider in an employment agreement or handbook are:

- ✪   what the salary and other compensation will be;

- ✪   what the hours of employment will be;

- ✪   what the probationary period will be;

- ✪   the sexual harassment policy;

- ✪   that the employee cannot sign any contracts binding the employer; and,

- ✪   that the employee agrees to arbitration rather than filing a lawsuit in the event of a dispute.

# Independent Contractors

One way to avoid problems with employees and taxes at the same time is to have all of your work done through *independent contractors*. This can relieve you of most of the burdens of employment laws and the obligation to pay Social Security and Medicare taxes for the workers.

An independent contractor is, in effect, a separate business that you pay to do a job. You pay them just as you pay any company from which you buy products or services. If the amount paid at the end of the year exceeds $600, you will issue an IRS Form 1099 instead of an IRS Form W-2.

This may seem too good to be true; and in some situations, it is. The IRS does not like independent contractor (IC) arrangements because it is too easy for the ICs to cheat on their taxes. To limit the use of ICs, the IRS has strict regulations on who may and may not be classified an independent contractor. Also, companies who do not appear to pay enough in wages for their field of business are often audited.

The highest at-risk jobs are those that are not traditionally done by independent contractors. For example, you could not get away with hiring a secretary as an independent contractor. One of the most important factors considered in determining if a worker can be an independent contractor is the amount of *control* the company has over his or her work. If you need someone to paint your building and you agree to pay them a certain price to do it according to their own methods and schedule, you can pay them as an independent contractor. But if you tell them when to work, how to do the job, and provide them with the tools and materials, they will be classified an employee.

If you just need some typing done and you take it to a typing service and pick it up when it is ready, you will be safe in treating them as independent contractors. But, if you need someone to come into your office to type on your machine at your schedule, you will probably be required to treat that person as an employee for tax purposes.

The IRS has a form you can use in determining if a person is an employee or an independent contractor, called **DETERMINATION OF EMPLOYEE WORK STATUS**. It is **IRS FORM SS-8** (see form 6, p.207).

**Independent Contractors versus Employees**

In deciding whether to make use of independent contractors or employees, you should weigh the following advantages and disadvantages.

*Advantages of using ICs.*

✪ *Lower taxes.* You do not have to pay Social Security, Medicare, unemployment, or other employee taxes.

✪ *Less paperwork.* You do not have to separate and then send federal withholding deposits or monthly employer returns to the state or federal government.

✪ *Less insurance.* You do not have to pay workers' compensation insurance and since the workers are not your employees, you do not have to insure against their possible liabilities.

✪ *More flexibility.* You can use ICs when you need them and not pay them when business is slow.

*Disadvantages of using ICs.*

✪ The IRS and state tax offices are strict about when workers may be qualified as ICs. They will audit companies whose use of ICs does not appear to be legitimate.

✪ If your use of ICs is found to be improper, you may have to pay back taxes and penalties and have problems with your pension plan.

✪ While employees usually cannot sue you for their injuries (if you have covered them with workers' compensation), ICs can sue you if their injuries were your fault.

✪ If you are paying someone to produce a creative work (writing, photography, artwork), you receive less rights to the work of an IC.

✪   You have less control over the work of an IC and less flexibility in terminating them if you are not satisfied that the job is being done the way you require.

✪   You have less loyalty from an IC who works sporadically for you and possibly others than from your own full time employees.

For some businesses, the advantages outweigh the disadvantages. For others, they do not. Consider your business plans and the consequences from each type of arrangement. Keep in mind that it will be easier to start with ICs and switch to employees than to hire employees and have to fire them to hire ICs.

# Temporary Workers

Another way to avoid the hassles of hiring employees is to get workers from a temporary agency. In this arrangement, you may pay a higher amount per hour for the work, but the agency will take care of all of the tax and insurance requirements. Since these can be expensive and time-consuming, the extra per hour cost may be well worth it.

Whether temporary workers will work for you depends upon the type of business you are in and the tasks you need performed. For such jobs as sales management, you would probably want someone who will stay with you long term and develop relationships with the buyers, but for order fulfillment, temporary workers might work out well.

Another advantage of temporary workers is that you can easily stop using those who do not work out well for you. Also, if you find one who is ideal, you may be able to hire him or her on a full-time basis.

In recent years, a new wrinkle has developed in the temporary worker area. Many large companies are beginning to use them because they are so much cheaper than paying the benefits demanded by full time employees. For example, Microsoft Corp. has had as many as 6,000 temporary workers, some of whom worked for them for years. However, some of the temporary workers recently won a lawsuit declaring that they are really employees and are entitled to the same benefits of other employees (such as pension plans).

The law is not yet settled in this area as to what arrangements will result in a temporary worker being declared an employee. That will take several more court cases, some of which have already been filed. A few things you can do to protect yourself include the following.

- ✪ Be sure that all of your benefit plans make it clear that they do not apply to workers obtained through temporary agencies.

- ✪ Do not keep the same temporary workers for longer than a year.

- ✪ Do not list temporary workers in any employee directories or hold them out to the public as your employees.

- ✪ Do not allow them to use your business cards or stationery.

## Firing Laws

In most cases, unless you have a contract with an employee for a set time period, you can fire him or her at any time for any or no reason. This is only fair since the employee can quit at any time. The exceptions to this are if you fired someone:

- ✪ based on illegal discrimination;

- ✪ for filing some sort of health or safety complaint; or,

- ✪ for refusing your sexual advances.

## Discrimination Laws

There are numerous federal laws forbidding discrimination based upon race, sex, pregnancy, color, religion, national origin, age, or disability. The laws apply to both hiring and firing and to employment practices such as salaries, promotions, and benefits. Most of these laws only apply to an employer who has fifteen or more employees for twenty weeks of a calendar year or has federal contracts or subcontracts. Therefore, you most likely will not be required to comply with the law immediately upon opening your business. However, there are similar state laws that may apply to your business.

One exception is the *Equal Pay Act* that applies to employers with two or more employees and requires that women be paid the same as men in the same type of job.

Employers with fifteen or more employees are required to display a poster regarding discrimination. This poster is available from the Equal Employment Opportunity Commission by calling 800-669-3362 or on their website at **www.dol.gov/esa/regs/compliance/posters/eeo.htm**. Employers with 100 or more employees are required to file an annual report with the EEOC.

***Discriminatory Interview Questions***

When hiring employees, some questions are illegal or inadvisable to ask. The following questions should not be included on your employment application, or in your interviews, unless the information is somehow directly tied to the duties of the job.

- ✪ Do not ask about an applicant's citizenship or place of birth. But after hiring an employee you must ask about his or her right to work in this country.

- ✪ Do not ask a female applicant her maiden name. You can ask if she has been known by any other name in order to do a background check.

- ✪ Do not ask if applicants have children, plan to have them, or have child care. You can ask if an applicant will be able to work the required hours.

- ✪ Do not ask if the applicant has religious objections to working Saturday or Sunday. You can mention if the job requires such hours and ask whether the applicant can meet this job requirement.

- ✪ Do not ask an applicant's age. You can ask if an applicant is eighteen or over, or for a liquor-related job if they are twenty-one or over.

- ✪ Do not ask an applicant's weight.

- ✪ Do not ask if an applicant has AIDS or is HIV positive.

✪ Do not ask if the applicant has filed a workers' compensation claim.

✪ Do not ask about the applicant's previous health problems.

✪ Do not ask if the applicant is married or whether his or her spouse would object to the job, hours, or duties.

✪ Do not ask if the applicant owns a home, furniture, or car, as it is considered racially-discriminatory.

✪ Do not ask if the applicant was ever arrested. You can ask if the applicant was ever convicted of a crime.

**ADA**    Under the *Americans with Disabilities Act* (ADA) of 1990, employers who do not make *reasonable accommodations* for disabled employees will face fines of up to $100,000, as well as other civil penalties and civil damage awards.

While the goal of creating more opportunities for people with disabilities is a good one, the result of this law is to place all of the costs of achieving this goal on businesses that are faced with disabled applicants. In fact, studies have shown that employers have hired fewer rather than more disabled people. It is theorized that this may be due to the expense of the reasonable accommodations or the fear of lawsuits by disabled employees.

The ADA currently applies to employers with fifteen or more employees. Employers who need more than fifteen employees might want to consider contracting with independent contractors to avoid problems with this law, particularly if the number of employees is only slightly larger than fifteen.

To find out how this law affects your business, you might want to pay the government $25 for its ADA Technical Assistance Manual. You can order it from:

**The Superintendent of Documents**
P.O. Box 371954
Pittsburgh, PA 15250-7954

You can also fax your credit card order to 202-512-2233.

*Tax benefits.* There are three types of tax credits to help small business with the burden of these laws.

✪ Businesses can deduct up to $15,000 a year for making their premises accessible to the disabled and can depreciate the rest (Internal Revenue Code Sec. 190).

✪ Small businesses (under $1,000,000 in revenue and under thirty employees) can get a tax credit each year for fifty percent of the cost of making their premises accessible to the disabled, but this only applies to the amount between $250 and $10,500.

✪ Small businesses can get a credit of up to forty percent of the first $6,000 of wages paid to certain new employees who qualify. See IRS form 8850 and instructions.

*Records.* To protect against potential claims of discrimination, all employers should keep detailed records showing reasons for hiring or not hiring applicants and for firing employees.

**Massachusetts Law**

Massachusetts has its own laws regarding discrimination in employment practices. Chapter 151B of the Massachusetts General Laws, which applies to employers with six or more employees, prohibits discrimination or classification based upon race, color, religion, sex, national origin, age, sexual orientation (excluding persons whose sexual orientation involves minor children as the sex object), ancestry, handicap, or marital status, unless based on a bona fide occupational qualification. It is also unlawful to require someone, as a condition of obtaining or keeping employment, to violate or forgo the practice of his creed or religion, including the observance of any particular holy day. Reasonable accommodation by the employer is required. An employer who violates these laws can be sued and be required to pay back pay, damages, and punitive damages.

# Sexual Harassment

What began as protection for employees who were fired or not promoted for failing to succumb to sexual advances of their superiors has been expanded to outlaw nearly any sexual comments or references in the workplace.

In the 1980's, the *Equal Employment Opportunity Commission* (EEOC) interpreted *Title VII* of the *Civil Rights Act of 1964* to forbid sexual harassment. After that, the courts took over and reviewed all types of conduct in the workplace. The numerous lawsuits that followed began a trend toward expanding the definition of sexual harassment and favoring employees.

The EEOC has held the following in sexual harassment cases.

- ✪ The victim as well as the harasser may be a woman or a man.

- ✪ The victim does not have to be of the opposite sex.

- ✪ The harasser can be the victim's supervisor, an agent of the employer, a supervisor in another area, a co-worker, or a non-employee.

- ✪ The victim does not have to be the person harassed, but could be anyone affected by the offensive conduct.

- ✪ Unlawful sexual harassment may occur without economic injury to or discharge of the victim.

- ✪ The harasser's conduct must be unwelcome.

Some of the actions that have been considered harassment are:

- ✪ displaying sexually explicit posters in the workplace;

- ✪ requiring female employees to wear revealing uniforms;

- ✪ rating the sexual attractiveness of female employees as they passed male employees' desks;

- ✪ continued sexual jokes and innuendos;

- ✪ demands for sexual favors from subordinates;

- ✪ unwelcomed sexual propositions or flirtation;

- ✪ unwelcomed physical contact; and,

- ✪ whistling or leering at members of the opposite sex.

In 1993, the United States Supreme Court ruled that an employee can make a claim for sexual harassment even without proof of a specific injury. However, lower federal courts in more recent cases have dismissed cases where no specific injury was shown. These new cases may indicate that the pendulum has stopped moving toward expanded rights for the employee.

On the other hand, another recent case ruled that an employer can be liable for the harassment of an employee by a supervisor, even if the employer was unaware of the supervisor's conduct, if the employer did not have a system in place to allow complaints against harassment. This area of law is still developing and to avoid a possible lawsuit you should be aware of the things that could potentially cause liability and avoid them.

Some things a business can do to protect against claims of sexual harassment are:

- ✪  distribute a written policy against all kinds of sexual harassment to all employees (this is required in Massachusetts);

- ✪  encourage employees to report all incidents of sexual harassment;

- ✪  ensure there is no retaliation against those who complain;

- ✪  make clear that your policy is *zero tolerance*;

- ✪  explain that sexual harassment includes both requests for sexual favors and a work environment that some employees may consider hostile;

- ✪  allow employees to report harassment to someone other than their immediate supervisor in case that person is involved in the harassment; and,

- ✪  promise as much confidentiality as possible to complainants.

**Massachusetts Law**    Massachusetts requires all employers with six or more employees to adopt a written policy against sexual harassment. The written policy must include:

- ✪  a statement that sexual harassment in the workplace is unlawful;

- ✪  a statement that it is unlawful to retaliate against an employee for filing a complaint of sexual harassment or for cooperating in an investigation of a complaint for sexual harassment;

✪ a description and examples of sexual harassment;

✪ a statement of the range of consequences for employees who are found to have committed sexual harassment;

✪ a description of the process for filing internal complaints about sexual harassment and the work addresses and telephone numbers of the person or persons to whom complaints should be made; and,

✪ the identity of the appropriate state and federal employment discrimination enforcement agencies and directions as to how to contact them.

Employers must provide all new employees with a copy of the policy when they commence employment and must provide each employee a copy annually. The law required the Massachusetts Commission Against Discrimination to prepare a model policy that conforms with the federal and state requirements.

***Common Law***   Although the federal and civil rights laws only apply to businesses with fifteen or more employees, and the Massachusetts laws to businesses with six or more employees, any employee could sue for sexual harassment in civil court. However, this is difficult, expensive, and would only be worthwhile when there were substantial damages.

# Wage and Hour Laws

The *Fair Labor Standards Act* (FLSA) applies to all employers who are engaged in *interstate commerce* or in the production of goods for interstate commerce (anything that will cross the state line) and all employees of hospitals, schools, residential facilities for the disabled or aged, or public agencies. It also applies to all employees of enterprises that gross $500,000 or more per year.

While many small businesses might not think they are engaged in interstate commerce, the laws have been interpreted so broadly that nearly any use of the mails, interstate telephone service, or other interstate services, however minor, is enough to bring a business under the law.

**Minimum Wage**    The federal wage and hour laws are contained in the Federal Fair Labor Standards Act. At the time this book was printed, the minimum wage is $5.15 per hour. In certain circumstances, a wage of $3.62 may be paid to employees under twenty years of age for a ninety day training period. For employees who regularly receive more than $30 a month in tips, the minimum wage is $2.13 per hour. But if the employee's tips do not bring him up to the full $5.15 minimum wage, then the employer must make up the difference.

**Overtime**    The general rule is that employees who work more than 40 hours a week must be paid time-and-a-half for hours worked over forty. But there are many exemptions to this general rule based on salary and position. These exceptions were completely revised in 2004 and an explanation of the changes including a tutorial video are available at www.dol.gov/esa. For answers to questions about the law, you can call the Department of Labor at 866-487-9243.

**Exempt Employees**    While nearly all businesses are covered, certain employees are exempt from the FLSA. Exempt employees include employees that are considered executives, administrative, managerial, professionals, computer professionals, and outside salespeople.

Whether one of these exceptions applies to a particular employee is a complicated legal question. Thousands of court cases have been decided on this issue but they have given no clear answers. In one case a person could be determined to be exempt because of his or her duties, but in another, a person with the same duties could be found not exempt.

One thing that is clear is that the determination is made on the employee's function, and not just the job title. You cannot make a secretary exempt by calling him or her a manager if most of the job duties are clerical. For more information see the Department of Labor website at **www.dol.gov/esa/whd/ flsa/index.htm.**

You can also obtain information on the Department of Labor's Employment Plan Guide at **www.dol.gov/asp/programs/guide.htm**.

**Massachusetts Law**    Massachusetts requires a minimum wage of $6.75 per hour, except in particular specified occupations. The Commissioner of Labor may set lower minimum rates for certain occupations, but may not set a rate lower than a specified amount per hour except for learners, apprentices, ushers, ticket sellers and takers, janitors, caretakers, golf caddies, and service people earning more than $20 a month in tips.

Most employees are entitled to time-and-a-half for hours worked over forty per week. Most employers must pay wages at least every two weeks, or pay no later than six days after the last day worked.

State, county, and certain municipal employees may not work more than eight hours a day, forty-eight hours a week, and six days a week, except in case of emergency.

Private employers must give employees in certain occupations twenty-four consecutive hours to rest every seven consecutive days. There are also restrictions on requiring employees to work on Sundays or holidays. Generally, employers must allow a thirty minute meal break for each six hours of work.

# Pension and Benefit Laws

There are no laws requiring small businesses to provide any types of special benefits to employees. Such benefits are given to attract and keep good employees. With pension plans the main concern is if you do start one it must comply with federal tax laws.

***Holidays***   There are no federal or Massachusetts laws that require that employees be given holidays off. You can require them to work Thanksgiving and Christmas and dock their pay or fire them for failing to show. Of course, you will not have much luck keeping employees with such a policy.

Most companies give full time employees a certain number of paid holidays, such as: New Year's Day (January 1); Memorial Day (last Monday in May); Fourth of July; Labor Day (first Monday in September); Thanksgiving (fourth Thursday in November); and, Christmas (December 25). Some employers include other holidays such as Martin Luther King, Jr.'s birthday (January 15); President's Day; and, Columbus Day. If one of the holidays falls on a Saturday or Sunday, many employers give the preceding Friday or following Monday off. Massachusetts law says that legal holidays include the following (or the day following when any of said days occurs on Sunday):

| | |
|---|---|
| New Year's Day | (January 1) |
| Martin Luther King, Jr.'s Birthday | (3rd Monday in January) |
| George Washington's Birthday | (3rd Monday in February) |
| Patriot's Day | (3rd Monday in April) |
| Memorial Day | (last Monday in May) |
| Independence Day | (July 4) |
| Labor Day | (1st Monday in September) |
| Columbus Day | (2nd Monday in October) |
| Veteran's Day | (November 11) |
| Thanksgiving Day | (4th Thursday in November) |
| Christmas Day | (December 25) |

With respect to Suffolk County only, Evacuation Day on March 17th (for certain purposes only) and Bunker Hill Day on June 17th, or the day following when said days occur on Sunday, are also legal holidays.

However, the fact that these are designated state holidays does not mean that private employers, other than owners of mills and factories, must observe them. In fact, not even the state government is closed on all of these days.

**Sick Days**  There is no federal or Massachusetts law mandating that an employee be paid for time that he or she is home sick. The situation seems to be that the larger the company, the more paid sick leave is allowed. Part-time workers rarely get sick leave and small business sick leave is usually limited for the simple reason that they cannot afford to pay for time that employees do not work.

Some small companies have an official policy of no paid sick leave, but when an important employee misses a day because he or she is clearly sick, it is paid.

**Pension Plans and Retirement Accounts**  Few small new businesses can afford to provide pension plans for their employees. The first concern of many small business owners is usually how the owner can shelter income in a pension plan without having to set up a pension plan for an employee. Under most pension plans, this is not allowed.

*IRA.* Anyone with $3,000 of earnings can put up to that amount in an Individual Retirement Account (IRA). Unless the person or his or her spouse is covered by a company pension plan and has income over a certain amount, the amount put into the account is fully tax deductible.

*ROTH IRA.* Contributions to a Roth IRA are not tax deductible but when the money is taken out, it is not taxable. People who expect to still have taxable income when they withdraw from their IRA can benefit from these.

*SEP IRA, SAR-SEP IRA, SIMPLE IRA.* With these types of retirement accounts, a person can put a much greater amount into a retirement plan and deduct it from their taxable income. Employees must also be covered by such plans, but certain employees are exempt so it is sometimes possible to use these for the owners alone. The best source for more information is a mutual fund company (such as Vanguard, Fidelity, Dreyfus, etc.) or a local bank, which can set up the plan and provide you with all of the rules. These have an advantage over qualified plans (discussed later) since they do not have the high annual fees. One Internet site that contains some useful information on these accounts is **www.retirement-information.com/iraaccts.htm.**

*Qualified Retirement Plans.* Qualified retirement plans are 401(k) plans, Keough plans, and corporate retirement plans. These are covered by ERISA, the *Employee Retirement Income Security Act.* ERISA is a complicated law meant to protect employee pension plans. Congress did not want employees who contributed to pension plans all their lives ending up with nothing when the plan goes bankrupt. The law is complicated and the penalties severe. However, many banks and mutual funds have created *canned plans* that can be used instead of drafting one from scratch. Still the fees for administering them are steep. Check with a bank or mutual fund for details.

# Family and Medical Leave Law

The *Family and Medical Leave Act of 1993* (FEML) requires an employee to be given up to twelve weeks of unpaid leave when:

- ✪ the employee or employee's spouse has a child;

- ✪ the employee adopts a child or takes in a foster child;

- ✪ the employee needs to care for an ill spouse, child, or parent; or,

- ✪ the employee becomes seriously ill.

The law only applies to employers with fifty or more employees. Also, the top 10% of an employer's salaried employees can be denied this leave because of the disruption in business their absence could cause.

**Massachusetts Law**

Massachusetts law requires employers with six or more employees to give up to eight weeks of maternity leave (but does not require pay during the period) for female employees for the purpose of giving birth or adopting a child under eighteen years of age, or under twenty-three years of age if mentally or physically disabled, provided the employee gives at least two weeks' notice and intends to return to work. Notice of this provision must be posted in the workplace.

Employees of manufacturing, mechanical, or mercantile establishments must be given leave to vote in any election during the first two hours after the polls are open, upon request. The law also requires leave in certain circumstances for training for armed forces reserves, participation in Veteran's Day or Memorial Day exercises, and jury duty.

In August of 1998, a new statute became effective in Massachusetts, entitled *An Act Providing Employee Leave for Certain Family Obligations*. The Act, commonly referred to as the Small Necessities Leave Act (SNLA), is applicable only to employers who are covered by the federal Family and Medical Leave Act of 1993.

The SNLA grants an eligible employee up to twenty-four hours of leave during any twelve-month period, in addition to leave under the FMLA, to:

✪ participate in school activities directly related to the educational advancement of a son or daughter of the employee, such as parent-teacher conferences or interviewing for a new school;

✪ accompany the son or daughter of the employee to routine medical or dental appointments, such as check-ups or vaccinations; or,

✪ accompany an elderly relative of the employee to routine medical or dental appointments or appointments for other professional services related to the elder's care, such as interviewing at nursing or group homes.

An elderly relative is defined as someone at least sixty years of age who is related by blood or marriage to the employee. A school is defined as a public or private elementary or secondary school, a Head Start program, or a state-licensed children's daycare facility.

There are various options to employers for determining the twelve month period and certain notice requirements.

# Child Labor Laws

The Federal Fair Labor Standards Act also contains rules regarding the hiring of children. The basic rules are that children under sixteen years old may not be hired at all except in a few jobs such as acting and newspaper delivery, and those under eighteen may not be hired for dangerous jobs. Children may not work more than three hours a day/eighteen hours a week in a school week or more than eight hours a day/forty hours a week in a nonschool week. If you plan to hire children, you should check the Federal Fair Labor Standards Act, in Chapter 29, United States Code (29 USC) and also the related regulations found in Chapter 29 of the Code of Federal Regulations (29 C.F.R.).

*Massachusetts Law*

Massachusetts also has its own child labor laws. The following rules apply to child labor in Massachusetts in addition to federal laws.

✪ Persons under eighteen generally may not work more than nine hours a day, forty-eight hours a week, or six days a week. In most cases, a child's hours of work each day must fall within ten consecutive hour period. These rules do not apply to professional, executive, administrative, supervisory, and personal secretarial positions.

✪ 16- and 17-year-olds can work only between 6 a.m. and 10 p.m., except in restaurants; they may also work in restaurants until midnight on Fridays, Saturdays, and during school vacations, except the last day of vacation; generally, they cannot work more than forty-eight hours a week, nine hours a day, or six days a week.

✪ 14- and 15-year olds can work only between 7 a.m. and 7 p.m. during the school year, and between 7 a.m. and 9 p.m. during the summer, and not during school hours; generally, they cannot work more than eighteen hours a week, three hours a day on school days, eight hours a day on Saturdays, Sundays, and holidays, or six days a week.

✪ Children are allowed to work up to fifty-two hours per week in certain types of seasonal employment from June to October.

- ✪ Children fourteen or younger may work in agricultural labor for up to four hours a day or twenty-four hours a week, or more if related to the owner or operator of farm.

- ✪ Children under sixteen may not work on certain equipment and in certain hazardous, arduous, or corruptive occupations, or in occupations that may unduly interfere with their schooling.

*Hazardous occupations.* No persons under eighteen years of age may work in the following occupations or use the following equipment:

- ✪ blast furnaces;

- ✪ hoisting machines;

- ✪ oiling or cleaning hazardous machinery in motion;

- ✪ polishing or buffing wheels;

- ✪ switch tending;

- ✪ gate tending;

- ✪ track repairing;

- ✪ brakeman, fireman, engineer, motorman, or conductor on railroad;

- ✪ fireman or engineer on boat;

- ✪ operating motor vehicles except in auto repair shop;

- ✪ gunpowder and other explosive manufacturing;

- ✪ manufacture of phosphorus or phosphorous matches;

- ✪ distillery, brewery or other bottling, manufacturing, or packing of alcoholic beverages;

- ✪ logging or sawmilling;

- ✪ selling alcoholic beverages;

- ✪ at heights of more than thirty feet above the floor of a room or above ground or water level; or,

- ✪ operating, cleaning, or repairing elevators.

# Immigration Laws

A law was passed in 1986 by Congress that imposes stiff penalties for any business that hires aliens who are not eligible to work. Under this law, you must verify both the identity and the employment eligibility of anyone you hire by using an **EMPLOYMENT ELIGIBILITY VERIFICATION (FORM I-9)**. (see form 4, p.195.) Both you and the employee must fill out the form and you must check an employee's identification cards or papers. Fines for hiring illegal aliens range from $250 to $2,000 for the first offense and up to $10,000 for the third offense. Failure to maintain the proper paperwork may result in a fine of up to $1,000. The law does not apply to independent contractors with whom you may contract, and it does not penalize you if the employee used fake identification.

There are also penalties that apply to employers of four or more persons for discriminating against eligible applicants because they appear foreign or because of their national origin or citizenship status.

Appendix A includes a sample filled-in **FORM I-9**. A blank form is in Appendix B.

For more information, call 202-514-2000 for the Handbook for Employers and Instructions for Completing Form I-9, check the Citizenship and Immigration Services website at **www.uscis.gov**.

**Massachusetts Law**    Massachusetts General Laws, Chapter 149, Section 19C makes it illegal to hire aliens who are not legally authorized to work.

# Hiring *Off the Books*

Because of the taxes, insurance, and red tape involved with hiring employees, some new businesses hire people *off the books*. They pay them in cash and never admit they are employees. While the cash paid in wages would not be deductible, they consider this a smaller cost than compliance. Some even use *off the books* receipts to cover it.

Except when your spouse or child is giving you some temporary help, this is a terrible idea. Hiring people off the books can result in civil fines, loss of insurance coverage, and even criminal penalties. When engaged in dangerous work like roofing or using power tools, you are risking millions of dollars in potential liability if a worker is killed or seriously injured.

It may be more costly and time consuming to comply with the employment laws, but if you are concerned about long-term growth with less risk, it is the wiser way to go.

# Federal Contracts

Companies that do work for the federal government are subject to several laws.

The *Davis-Bacon Act* requires contractors engaged in U.S. government construction projects to pay wages and benefits that are equal to or better than the prevailing wages in the area.

The *McNamara-O'Hara Service Contract Act* sets wages and other labor standards for contractors furnishing services to agencies of the U.S. government.

The *Walsh-Healey Public Contracts Act* requires the Department of Labor to settle disputes regarding manufacturers supplying products to the U.S. government.

# Miscellaneous Laws

*Affirmative action.* In most cases, the federal government does not yet tell employers who they must hire. This would be especially true for small new businesses. The only situation where a small business would need to comply with affirmative action requirements would be if it accepted federal contracts or subcontracts. These requirements could include the hiring of minorities or Vietnam veterans.

*Layoffs.* Companies with one hundred or more full-time employees at one location are subject to the *Worker Adjustment and Retraining Notification Act.* This law requires a sixty-day notification prior to certain lay-offs and has other strict provisions.

*Unions.* The *National Labor Relations Act of 1935* gives employees the right to organize a union or to join one. (29 U.S.C., Sec. 151 et seq.) There are things employers can do to protect themselves, but consult a labor attorney or a book on the subject before taking action that might be illegal and result in fines.

*Poster laws.* There are laws regarding what posters you are required to display. The following list should be of help.

✪ All employers must display the wage and hour poster available from:
**U. S. Department of Labor**
www.dol.gov/esa

✪ Employers with fifteen or more employees for twenty weeks of the year must display the sex, race, religion, and ethnic discrimination poster and the age discrimination poster available from:
**EEOC**
www.eeoc.gov/publications.html

✪ Employers with federal contracts or subcontracts of $10,000 or more must display the sex, race, etc. discrimination poster  mentioned above plus a poster regarding Vietnam era veterans available from the local federal contracting office.

✪ Employers with government contracts subject to the *Service Contract Act* or the *Public Contracts Act* must display a notice to employees working on government contracts available from:

**Employment Standards Division**

www.dol.gov/esa

**Massachusetts Law**

*Working conditions.* Employers must provide proper ventilation, sanitation, lighting, and heat from October 15 to May 15. Industrial and construction workers must be provided drinking water. Fire exits must be accessible during working hours.

*Personnel records.* Employers must, upon written request of present and former employees, allow those persons to inspect and copy their personnel records.

*Prevention of employment.* No one may, by intimidation or force, prevent or seek to prevent a person from entering into or continuing in the employment of any person.

*Coercion of agreement not to join a labor organization.* No one may coerce or compel a person into an agreement not to join or become a member of a labor organization as a condition of securing employment or continuing employment.

*Volunteer experience.* Employment applications requiring the applicant to set forth experience history must contain a statement that the applicant may include in such history any verified work performed on a volunteer basis.

*Seats.* Employers must provide seats for employees and must allow their use when not engaged in active duties of employment and while at work unless sitting would interfere with the work or cause danger.

# II | ADVERTISING AND PROMOTION LAWS

Federal rules do not apply to every business. Small businesses that operate only within one state and do not use the postal service may be exempt. However, many of the federal rules are encompassed by Massachusetts' unfair trade practices laws. Therefore, a violation could be prosecuted by the state rather than the federal government.

## Advertising Laws and Rules

The federal government regulates advertising through the *Federal Trade Commission* (FTC). The rules are contained in the *Code of Federal Regulations* (C.F.R.). You can find these rules in most law libraries and many public libraries. If you plan any advertising that you think may be questionable, you might want to check the rules. If you question it, most likely the Washington bureaucrats have forbidden it.

***Deceptive Pricing***      When prices are being compared, it is required that actual and not inflated prices are used. For example, if an object would usually be sold for $7, you should not first offer it for $10 and then start offering it at thirty percent off. It is considered misleading to suggest that a discount from list price is a bargain if the item is seldom actually sold at list price. If most surrounding stores sell an item for $7, it is considered misleading to say it has a *retail value of $10* even if there are some stores elsewhere selling it at that price. (16 C.F.r. Part 233.)

**Bait Advertising**

*Bait advertising* is placing an ad when you do not really want the respondents to buy the product offered, but to switch to another item. The factors used to determine if there was a violation are similar to those used by Massachusetts in applying its unfair trade practices laws. (16 C.F.R. Part 238.)

*Use of* **free, half-off,** *and similar words.* Use of words such as *free, 1¢ sale,* and the like must not be misleading. This means that the *regular price* must not include a mark-up to cover the *free* item. The seller must expect to sell the product without the free item at some time in the future. (16 C.F.R. Part 251.)

**Substantiation of Claims**

The FTC requires that advertisers be able to substantiate their claims. Some information on this policy is contained on the Internet at **www.ftc.gov/bcp/ guides/ad3subst.htm**. (16 C.F.R. Sec. 3.40 and 48 F.R. Page 10471 (1983).)

**Endorsements**

This rule forbids endorsements that are misleading. An example is a quote from a film review used in such a way as to change the substance of the review. It is not necessary to use the exact words of the person endorsing the product as long as the opinion is not distorted. If a product is changed, an endorsement that does not apply to the new version cannot be used. For some items, such as drugs, claims cannot be used without scientific proof. Endorsements by organizations cannot be used unless one is sure that the membership holds the same opinion. (16 C.F.R. Part 255.)

**Unfairness**

Any advertising practices that can be deemed to be *unfair* are forbidden by the FTC. An explanation of this policy is located on the Internet at **www.ftc.gov/ bcp/policystmt/ad-unfair.htm**. (15 U.S.C. Sec. 45.)

**Negative Option Plans**

When a seller uses a sales system in which the buyer must notify the seller if he or she does not want the goods, the seller must provide the buyer with a form to decline the sale and at least ten days in which to decline. Bonus merchandise must be shipped promptly and the seller must promptly terminate any who so request after completion of the contract. (16 C.F.R. Part 425.)

**Food and Dietary Supplements**

Under the *Nutritional Labeling Education Act of 1990*, the FTC and the FDA regulate the packaging and advertising of food and dietary products. Anyone involved in this area should obtain a copy of these rules. They are located on the Internet at **www.ftc.gov/bcp/menu-health.htm#bized.** and **www.ftc.gov/bcp/ guides/ad-food.htm**. (21 U.S.C. Sec. 343.)

*Jewelry and precious metals.* The FTC has numerous rules governing the sale and advertising of jewelry and precious metals. Anyone in this business should obtain a copy of these rules. They are located on the Internet at **www.ftc.gov/ bcp/guides/jewel-gd.htm**. (61 C.F.R. Sec. 27212.)

***Massachusetts Laws***

Massachusetts has unfair trade practices laws that provide for treble damages for consumers against businesses that have willfully or knowingly violated the law. Among the prohibited actions are the following.

- ✪ Advertising goods at less than cost plus sales tax for the purpose of injuring or destroying competition (with exceptions).

- ✪ Failure by a merchant to disclose any fact, the disclosure of which may have influenced the buyer not to enter into the transaction to start with.

- ✪ Failure by a merchant in advertising to disclose all material facts concerning the product or service that, if not disclosed, might directly or by implication, mislead the consumer.

- ✪ Making any claim or representation by any means has the capacity or tendency or effect of deceiving buyers or prospective buyers as to the value or the past, present, common, or usual price of a product, or as to any reduction in price of a product, or any saving relating to a product.

- ✪ A statement or illustration in an advertisement that creates a false impression of the grade, quality, make, value, currency of model, size, color, usability, or origin of the product offered, or which may otherwise misrepresent the product in such a manner that later, on disclosure of the true facts, there is a likelihood that the buyer may be switched from the advertised product to another.

- ✪ Engaging in any act or practice to discourage the purchase of the advertised product as part of a bait scheme to sell another product.

- ✪ Car dealers forcing customers to purchase optional accessories installed by the dealer.

✪ Negligent misrepresentation of fact when the truth is reasonably capable of ascertainment. This might include the following things:

- misrepresenting the owner, manufacturer, distributor, source, or geographical origin of goods;

- misrepresenting the age, model, grade, style, or standard of goods;

- misrepresenting the sponsorship, endorsement, approval, or certification of goods or services;

- misrepresenting the affiliation, connection, or association of any goods or services;

- misrepresenting the nature, characteristics, standard ingredients, uses, benefits, warranties, guarantees, quantities, or qualities of goods or services;

- misrepresenting used, altered, deteriorated, or repossessed goods as new;

- disparaging goods, services, or business of another by false or misleading representation; or,

- advertising goods or services with intent not to sell them as advertised.

# Internet Sales Laws

There are not yet specific laws governing Internet transactions that are different from laws governing other transactions. The FTC feels that its current rules regarding deceptive advertising, substantiation, disclaimers, refunds, and related matters must be followed by Internet businesses and that consumers are adequately protected by them.

For some specific guidelines on Internet advertising, see the FTC's site at:
www.ftc.gov/bcp/conline/pubs/buspubs/ruleroad.htm

# Home Solicitation Laws

The Federal Trade Commission has rules governing door-to-door sales. It is a deceptive trade practice in any such sale to fail to furnish a receipt explaining the sale (in the language of the presentation). It is also deceptive not to give notice that there is a right to back out of the contract within three days, known as a *right of rescission*. The notice must be supplied in duplicate, must be in at least ten-point type, and must be captioned either *Notice of Right to Cancel* or *Notice of Cancellation*. The notice must be worded as follows on the next page.

NOTICE OF CANCELLATION

_____
Date

YOU MAY CANCEL THIS TRANSACTION, WITHOUT ANY PENALTY OR OBLIGATION, WITHIN THREE BUSINESS DAYS FROM THE ABOVE DATE.

IF YOU CANCEL, ANY PROPERTY TRADED IN, ANY PAYMENTS MADE BY YOU UNDER THE CONTRACT OR SALE, AND ANY NEGOTIABLE INSTRUMENT EXECUTED BY YOU WILL BE RETURNED TO YOU WITHIN 10 BUSINESS DAYS FOLLOWING RECEIPT BY THE SELLER OF YOUR CANCELLATION NOTICE, AND ANY SECURITY INTEREST ARISING OUT OF THE TRANSACTION WILL BE CANCELLED.

IF YOU CANCEL, YOU MUST MAKE AVAILABLE TO THE SELLER AT YOUR RESIDENCE, IN SUBSTANTIALLY AS GOOD CONDITION AS WHEN RECEIVED, ANY GOODS DELIVERED TO YOU UNDER THIS CONTRACT OR SALE; OR YOU MAY IF YOU WISH, COMPLY WITH THE INSTRUCTIONS OF THE SELLER REGARDING THE RETURN SHIPMENT OF THE GOODS AT THE SELLER'S EXPENSE AND RISK.

IF YOU DO MAKE THE GOODS AVAILABLE TO THE SELLER AND THE SELLER DOES NOT PICK THEM UP WITHIN 20 DAYS OF THE DATE OF YOUR NOTICE OF CANCELLATION, YOU MAY RETAIN OR DISPOSE OF THE GOODS WITHOUT ANY FURTHER OBLIGATION. IF YOU FAIL TO MAKE THE GOODS AVAILABLE TO THE SELLER, OR IF YOU AGREE TO RETURN THE GOODS AND FAIL TO DO SO, THEN YOU REMAIN LIABLE FOR PERFORMANCE OF ALL OBLIGATIONS UNDER THE CONTRACT.

TO CANCEL THIS TRANSACTION, MAIL OR DELIVER A SIGNED AND DATED COPY OF THIS CANCELLATION NOTICE OR ANY OTHER WRITTEN NOTICE, OR SEND A TELEGRAM, TO _____[name of seller], AT _____[address of seller's place of business] NOT LATER THAN MIDNIGHT OF _____ [date].

I HEREBY CANCEL THIS TRANSACTION.

_____     _____
(Buyer's signature)                                                      (Date)

The seller must complete the notice and orally inform the buyer of the right to cancel. He or she cannot misrepresent the right to cancel, assign the contract until the fifth business day, nor include a confession of judgment in the contract. For more specific details see the rules contained at 16 C.P.R. Part 429.

**Massachusetts Law**

Massachusetts also has laws allowing buyers to cancel certain transactions within three days and requiring the seller or lessor to give written notice of this right. Covered transactions are those that are:

✪ consumer transactions (sales, rental, lease);

✪ over $25 (including all charges, interest, etc.);

✪ primarily for personal, family, or household purposes; and,

✪ consummated other than at the seller's regular place of business.

*Right to cancel.* Any such sale described above my be cancelled by the buyer by written notice postmarked any time before midnight of the third business day after the sales day.

*Written agreement.* Every such sale must be in writing and must contain the following notice in bold face type and at least ten point size.

> **You may cancel this agreement if it has been signed by a party thereto at a place other than an address of the seller, which may be his main office or branch thereof, provided you notify the seller in writing at his main office or branch by ordinary mail posted, by telegram sent or by delivery, not later than midnight of the third business day following the signing of this agreement. See the attached notice of cancellation form for an explanation of this right.**

Attached to the notice must be a form in duplicate that is easily detachable, stating the same, in at least ten point boldface type, as the federal notice reproduced on the previous page.

*Seller's duty.* All businesses conducting solicitation sales must:

✪ ensure that all employees have the required permits;

✪ register with the chief of police or other designated official of a town or city; and,

✪ notify the chief of police or other designated official in each town where sales are to be made.

# Telephone Solicitation Laws

*Phone calls.* In 2003 the Federal Trade Commission issued new rules regulating telephone solicitation calls. The main provision of these rules allow consumers to be listed on a national *Do Not Call* registry and any company that calls those on the list is subject to penalties. Other provisions:

✪ require disclosures of specific information;

✪ prohibit misrepresentations;

✪ limit when telemarketers may call consumers;

✪ require transmission of Caller ID information;

✪ prohibit abandoned outbound calls, subject to a safe harbor;

✪ prohibit unauthorized billing;

✪ set payment restrictions for the sale of certain goods and services; and,

✪ require that specific business records be kept for two years.

For more information on these rules you can visit **www.telemarketing. donotcall.gov**. If you have questions about the rules you can call 202-326-3737 or email them at **tsrquestions@ftc.gov**.

*Faxes.* It is illegal under the act to send advertising faxes to anyone who has not consented to receiving such faxes or is an existing customer.

***Massachusetts Law***

In Massachusetts, with respect to telephone solicitations, the person calling must, before making any other statement except a greeting and before asking any questions, state the identity of the caller, the trade name of the person represented by the caller, and the kind of goods or services being offered for sale. Callers using automatic dialing systems may not call those who have given notice to their telephone company that they do not want to receive those calls.

*Automatic dialing.* All telephone customers have the right to notify the telephone company that they do not wish to receive telephone calls from an automatic dialing system. The phone company cannot charge for this service.

# Pricing, Weights, and Labeling

Beginning in 1994, all food products were required to have labels with information on the product's nutritional values such as calories, fat, and protein. For most products, the label must be in the required format so that consumers can easily compare products. However, if such a format will not fit on the product label, the information may be in another format that is easily readable.

***Massachusetts Law***

The rules also require metric measurement. Under these rules, metric measures do not have to be the first measurement on the container, but they must be included. Food items that are packaged as they are sold (such as delicatessen items) do not have to contain metric labels.

Massachusetts laws require that every item in food stores and every grocery item in food departments to be individually marked with the correct selling price. Many items are exempted, provided that a conspicuous separate sign indicated the price and that the cashier can readily discern the price of each item.

Massachusetts also has voluminous statutes governing the labeling requirements for a variety of specific items, including the following:

- ✪ horse meat;
- ✪ potatoes;
- ✪ farm products;
- ✪ native fruits, vegetables, and turkeys;
- ✪ artificial colorings and flavorings;
- ✪ preservatives;
- ✪ cosmetics;
- ✪ patent medicine or food; containing drugs;

- stuffed toys and furniture;
- furs;
- non-original paintings;
- sewing thread;
- poison;
- anti-freeze;
- electric appliances;
- hazardous substances;
- milk cans;
- canned soaked goods;
- honey;
- gold;
- kosher food;
- vinegar;
- prescription drugs;
- alcoholic beverages;
- safety glazing materials;
- explosives;
- frozen desserts;
- baking powder;
- livestock and poultry products;
- lard;
- process or renovated butter;
- imitation butter and cheeses;
- margarine;
- milk and cream;
- bottled water;
- bakery products;
- molasses;
- flammable clothing and fabrics;
- fertilizers;
- seeds;
- shellfish;
- halibut;
- unstable drugs;
- imitation foods; and,
- maple syrup and maple syrup food products.

# Email Advertising

The *Controlling the Assault of Nonsolicited Pornography and Marketing Act of 2003* (CANSPAM) has put numerous controls on how you can use email to solicit business for your company. Some of the prohibited activities under the Act are:

- false or misleading information in an email;

- deceptive subject heading;

- failure to include a functioning return address;

- mailing to someone who has asked not to receive solicitations;

- failure to include a valid postal address;

- omitting an opt-out procedure;

✪    failure to clearly mark the email as advertising; and,

✪    including sexual material without adequate warnings.

Some of the provisions contain criminal penalties as well as civil fines.

For more information on the CANSPAM Act see:
www.gigalaw.com/canspam

For text of the Act plus other spam laws around the world see:
www.spamlaws.com

# 12 PAYMENT AND COLLECTION

Depending on the business you are in, you may be paid by cash, checks, credit cards, or some sort of financing arrangement such as a promissory note and mortgage. Both state and federal laws affect the type of payments you collect and failure to follow the laws can cost you considerably.

## Cash

Cash is probably the easiest form of payment and it is subject to few restrictions. The most important one is that you keep an accurate accounting of your cash transactions and that you report all of your cash income on your tax return. Recent efforts to stop the drug trade have resulted in some serious penalties for failing to report cash transactions and for money laundering. The laws are so sweeping that even if you deal in cash in an ordinary business, you may violate the law and face huge fines and imprisonment.

The most important law to be concerned with is the one requiring the filing of IRS Form 8300 for cash transactions of $10,000 or more. A transaction does not have to happen in one day. If a person brings you smaller amounts of cash that add up to $10,000 and the government can construe them as one transaction, the form must be filed. Under this law, *cash* also includes travelers' checks and money orders, but not cashiers' checks or bank checks. For more information, obtain IRS Form 8300 and instructions from the IRS.

# Checks

It is important to accept checks in your business. While there is a small percentage that will be bad, most checks will be good and you will be able to accommodate more customers. To avoid having problems with checks, you should comply with the following rules.

*Accepting Checks*

A business cannot require a customer to provide a credit card number or expiration date in order to pay by check. (Massachusetts General Laws (Mass. Gen. Laws), Chapter (Ch.) 93, Section (Sec.) 105.) The business can request to see a card to establish that the customer is credit-worthy or for additional identification and can record the type of credit card and issuing company. However, the business cannot record the number of the card.

*Bad Checks*

Massachusetts has a fairly effective bad check collection process. If you follow the rules, you may be able to collect on a bad check. Call your local police department to find out how to proceed.

Be sure that you are able to identify the person who gave you the check. To do this, you should require identification and write down the sources of identification on the face of the check. Make sure they sign the check!

*Refunds After Cashing Check*

A popular scam is for a person to purchase something by using a check and then come back the next day demanding a refund. After making the refund, the business discovers the initial payment check bounced. Do not make refunds until checks clear!

# Credit Cards

In our buy-now, pay-later society, charge cards can add greatly to your sales potential, especially with large, discretionary purchases. For MasterCard, Visa, and Discover, the fees are about two percent, and this amount is easily paid for by the extra purchases that the cards allow. American Express charges four to five percent and you may decide this is not worth paying since almost everyone who has an American Express card also has another card.

For businesses that have a retail outlet, there is usually no problem getting merchant status. Most commercial banks can handle it. Discover can also set you up to accept their card, as well as MasterCard and Visa, and they will wire the money into your bank account daily.

For mail order businesses, especially those operating out of the home, it is much harder to get merchant status. This is because of the number of scams in which large amounts are charged, no products are shipped, and the company folds. One good thing about American Express is that they will accept mail order companies operating out of the home.

Some companies open a small storefront (or share one) to get merchant status, then process mostly mail orders. The processors usually do not want to accept you if you will do more than fifty percent mail order; but if you do not have many complaints, you may be allowed to process mostly mail orders. Whatever you do, keep your charge customers happy so that they do not complain!

You might be tempted to try to run your charges through another business. This may be okay if you actually sell your products through them, but if you run your business charges through their account, the other business may lose its merchant status. For example, if you are selling books and running credit card charges through your friend's florist shop account, people who buy a book by mail from you and then have a charge on their credit card statement from a florist shop will probably call the credit card company saying that they never bought anything from the florist shop. Too many of these and your friend's account for her florist shop will be closed.

# Financing Laws

Some businesses can make sales more easily if they finance the purchases themselves. If the business has enough capital to do this, it can earn extra profits on the financing terms. Nonetheless, because of abuses, many consumer protection laws have been passed by both the federal and state governments.

**Regulation Z**     Two important federal laws regarding financing are called the *Truth in Lending Act* and the *Fair Credit Billing Act*. These are implemented by what is called *Regulation Z* (commonly known as *Reg. Z*), issued by the Board of Governors of the Federal Reserve System. It is contained in Title 12 of the Code of Federal Regulations, page 226. (12 C.F.R. p.226.) This is a very complicated law, and some have said that no business can be sure to be in compliance with it.

The regulation covers all transactions in which all four of the following conditions are met:

1.  credit is offered;

2   the offering of credit is regularly done;

3.  there is a finance charge for the credit or there is a written agreement with more than four payments; and,

4.  the credit is for personal, family, or household purposes.

It also covers credit card transactions where only the first two conditions above are met. It applies to leases if the consumer ends up paying the full value and keeping the item leased. It does not apply to the following transactions:

✪  transactions with businesses or agricultural purposes;

✪  transactions with organizations such as corporations or the government;

✪  transactions of over $25,000 that are not secured by the consumer's dwelling;

✪  credit involving public utilities;

✪  credit involving securities or commodities; and,

✪  home fuel budget plans.

The way for a small business to avoid Reg. Z violations is to avoid transactions that meet the conditions or to make sure all transactions fall under the exceptions. This is easy for many businesses. Instead of extending credit to customers, accept credit cards and let the credit card company extend the credit. However, if your customers usually do not have credit cards or if you are in a business, such as used car sales, which often extends credit, consult a lawyer knowledgeable about Reg. Z or, if you dare, get a copy for yourself at: www.cardreport.com/laws/tila/tila.html

***Massachusetts Law***

Massachusetts also has extensive laws regarding financing arrangements. The law governs disclosure, cancellation provisions, and limitations on interest rates. Anyone engaged in installment sales in Massachusetts should carefully review the latest version of Massachusetts General Laws, Chapter 255D, Retail Installment Sales and Services. Chapter 255B, Retail Installment Sales of Motor Vehicles, may also be relevant.

In addition to these acts, Massachusetts forbids discrimination in granting credit based upon age, sex, sexual orientation, marital status, race, color, religion, national origin, children, handicap, or the fact that all or part of one's income comes from an assistance program.

# Usury

*Usury* is the charging of an illegally high rate of interest. In Massachusetts, the maximum rate of interest you may charge is twenty percent, unless you notify the attorney general and keep adequate records (what constitutes adequate records is not explained in the law).

# Collections

The *Fair Debt Collection Practices Act of 1977* bans the use of deception, harassment, and other unreasonable acts in the collection of debts. It has strict requirements whenever someone is collecting a debt for someone else (that is, they do not apply if you are collecting your own debt). If you are in the collection business (*i.e.*, you are in the business of collecting debts owed to others), you must get a copy of this law.

The Federal Trade Commission has issued some rules that prohibit deceptive representations such as pretending to be in the motion picture industry, the government, or a credit bureau, or using questionnaires that do not say that they are for the purpose of collecting a debt. (16 C.F.R. Part 237.)

**Massachusetts Law**

The *Unfair Debt Collection Practices Law* applies to debts owed by persons (not corporations) for transactions that were for personal, family, or household purposes. (Mass. Gen. Law., Ch. 93, Sec. 49.) The law forbids:

- ✪ using instruments that simulate judicial process;

- ✪ communicating with third parties about the debt without permission of the debtor;

- ✪ communicating with the debtor after being notified that communications should be directed to the debtor's attorney; and,

- ✪ harassing or embarrassing the debtor.

# 13 BUSINESS RELATIONS LAWS

There are many other laws that affect businesses generally. Some are very specific, while others are broad areas of concern. Review the laws discussed in this chapter against the type of business you wish to open to see if any apply to you.

## The Uniform Commercial Code

The *Uniform Commercial Code* (UCC) is a set of laws regulating numerous aspects of doing business. A national group drafted this set of uniform laws to avoid having a patchwork of different laws around the fifty states. Although some states modified some sections of the laws, the code is basically the same in most of the states. In Massachusetts, the UCC is contained in chapter 106 of Massachusetts General Laws. Each chapter is concerned with a different aspect of commercial relations such as sales, warranties, bank deposits, commercial paper, and bulk transfers.

Businesses that wish to know their rights in all types of transactions should obtain a copy of the UCC and become familiar with it. It is especially useful in transactions between merchants. However, the meaning is not always clear from a reading of the statutes. In many law schools, students spend a full semester studying each chapter of this law.

# Commercial Discrimination

The *Robinson-Patman Act of 1936* prohibits businesses from injuring competition by offering the same goods at different prices to different buyers. This means that the large chain stores should not be getting a better price than your small shop. It also requires that promotional allowances must be made on proportionally the same terms to all buyers.

As a small business, you may be a victim of Robinson-Patman Act violations. A good place to look for information on the act is at **www.lawmall.com/rpa**.

**Massachusetts Law**    Massachusetts' *Unfair Sales Act* makes unlawful the advertising, offer for sale, and sale of merchandise at less than cost with the *intent to injure competitors or destroy competition*.

# Restraining Trade

One of the earliest federal laws affecting business is the *Sherman Antitrust Act of 1890*. The purpose of the law was to protect competition in the marketplace by prohibiting monopolies. For example, one large company might buy out all of its competitors and then raise prices to astronomical levels. In recent years, this law was used to break up AT&T.

Examples of some things that are prohibited are:

- ✪ agreements between competitors to sell at the same prices;

- ✪ agreements between competitors on how much will be sold or produced;

- ✪ agreements between competitors to divide up a market;

✪ refusing to sell one product without a second product; and,

✪ exchanging information among competitors that results in similarity of prices.

As a new business, you probably will not be in a position to violate the Act, but you should be aware of it in case a larger competitor tries to put you out of business. A good place to find information on the act is at **www.lawmall.com/sherman.act.**

***Massachusetts Law***

Massachusetts anti-trust laws are substantially identical to federal laws. Where federal laws do not apply because interstate commerce is not involved, the Massachusetts laws would apply to business activities in Massachusetts.

# Intellectual Property Protection

As a business owner, you should know enough about intellectual property law to protect your own creations and to keep from violating the rights of others. Intellectual property is that which is the product of human creativity, such as writings, designs, inventions, melodies, and processes. They are things that can be stolen without being physically taken. For example, if you write a book, someone can steal the words from your book without stealing a physical copy of it.

As the Internet grows, intellectual property is becoming more valuable. Smart business owners are those who will take the action necessary to protect their company's intellectual property. Additionally, business owners should know intellectual property law to be sure that they do not violate the rights of others. Even an unknowing violation of the law can result in stiff fines and penalties.

The following are the types of intellectual property and the ways to protect them.

***Patent***

A *patent* is protection given to new and useful inventions, discoveries, and designs. To be entitled to a patent, a work must be completely new and *unobvious*. A patent is granted to the first inventor who files for the patent. Once an invention is patented, no one else can make use of that invention, even if they discover it independently after a lifetime of research. A patent protects an invention for seventeen years and protects designs for three-and-a-half, seven, or fourteen years. Patents cannot be renewed. The patent application must clearly explain how to make the invention so that when the patent expires, others will be able to freely make and use the invention. Patents are registered with the United States Patent and Trademark Office (USPTO). Examples of things which would be patentable would be mechanical devices or new drug formulas.

**Copyright**

A *copyright* is protection given to *original works of authorship*, such as written works, musical works, visual works, performance works, or computer software programs. A copyright exists from the moment of creation, but one cannot register a copyright until it has been fixed in tangible form. Also, one cannot copyright titles, names, or slogans. A copyright currently gives the author and his or her heirs exclusive right to the work for the life of the author plus seventy years. Copyrights first registered before 1978 last for ninety-five years. This was previously seventy-five years but was extended twenty years to match the European system. Copyrights are registered with the Register of Copyrights at the Library of Congress. Examples of works that would be copyrightable are books, paintings, songs, poems, plays, drawings, and films.

**Trademark**

A *trademark* is protection given to a name or symbol that is used to distinguish one person's goods or services from those of others. It can consist of letters, numerals, packaging, labeling, musical notes, colors, or a combination of these. If a trademark is used on services, as opposed to goods, it is called a *service mark*. A trademark lasts indefinitely if it is used continuously and renewed properly. Trademarks are registered with the United States Patent and Trademark Office and with individual states. This is explained further in Chapter 3.

**Trade Secrets**

A *trade secret* is some information or process that provides a commercial advantage, which is protected by keeping it a secret. Examples of trade secrets may be a list of successful distributors, the formula for Coca-Cola, or some unique source code in a computer program. Trade secrets are not registered anywhere, but are protected by the fact that they are not disclosed. They are protected only for as long as they are kept secret. If you independently discover the formula for Coca-Cola tomorrow, you can freely market it. (But you cannot use the trademark *Coca-Cola* on your product to market it.)

*Massachusetts law.* Massachusetts law provides that stealing trade secrets constitutes larceny. Penalties include fines of up to $25,000 and/or imprisonment.

**Nonprotectable Creations**

Some things are just not protectable. Such things as ideas, systems, and discoveries are not allowed any protection under any law. If you have a great idea, such as selling packets of hangover medicine in bars, you cannot stop others from doing the same thing. If you invent a new medicine, you can patent it; if you pick a distinctive name for it, you can register it as a trademark; if you create a unique picture or instructions for the package, you can copyright them. You cannot stop others from using your basic business idea of marketing hangover medicine in bars.

Notice the subtle differences between the protective systems available. If you invent something two days after someone else does, you cannot even use it yourself if the other person has patented it. But if you write the same poem as someone else and neither of you copied the other, both of you can copyright the poem. If you patent something, you can have the exclusive rights to it for the term of the patent, but you must disclose how others can make it after the patent expires. However, if you keep it a trade secret, you have exclusive rights as long as no one learns the secret.

# 14 ENDLESS LAWS

The Commonwealth of Massachusetts and the federal government have numerous laws and rules that apply to every aspect of every type of business. There are laws governing even such things as exploding golf balls and selling baby food at flea markets.

Some activities are covered by both state and federal laws. In such cases, you must obey the stricter of the rules. In addition, more than one agency of the state or federal government may have rules governing your business. Each of these may have the power to investigate violations and impose fines or other penalties.

Penalties for violations of these laws can range from a warning to a criminal fine and even jail time. In some cases, employees can sue for damages. It is your duty to learn which laws apply to your business or to risk these penalties.

Very few people in business know the laws that apply to their businesses. If you take the time to learn them, you can become an expert in your field and avoid problems with regulators. You can also fight back if one of your competitors uses some illegal method to compete with you.

The laws and rules that affect the most businesses are explained in this section. Following that is a list of more specialized laws. You should read through this list and see which ones may apply to your business. Then go to your public library or law library and read them. Some may not apply to your phase of the business, but if any of them do apply, make copies to keep on hand.

No one could possibly know all the rules that affect business, much less comply with them all. The Interstate Commerce Commission alone has forty trillion (that is forty million million or 40,000,000,000,000) rates on its books telling the transportation industry what it should charge! But if you keep up with the important rules, you will stay out of trouble and have more chance of success.

# Federal Laws

The federal laws which are most likely to affect small businesses are rules of the Federal Trade Commission (FTC). The FTC has some rules that affect many businesses such as the rules about labeling, warranties, and mail order sales. Other rules affect only certain industries.

If you sell goods by mail, you should send for their booklet, *A Business Guide to the Federal Trade Commission's Mail Order Rule*. If you are going to be involved in a certain industry, such as those listed below, or using warranties or your own labeling, you should ask for their latest information on the subject. The address is:

**Federal Trade Commission**
Consumer Response Center
600 Pennsylvania Avenue, NW
Washington, DC 20580

The rules of the FTC are contained in the Code of Federal Regulations (C.F.R) in Chapter 16. Some of the industries covered are:

| Industry | Part |
|---|---|
| Adhesive Compositions | 235 |
| Aerosol Products Used for Frosting Cocktail Glasses | 417 |
| Automobiles (New car fuel economy advertising) | 259 |
| Barber Equipment and Supplies | 248 |
| Binoculars | 402 |

| <u>Industry</u> | <u>Part</u> |
|---|---|
| Business Opportunities and Franchises | 436 |
| Cigarettes | 408 |
| Decorative Wall Paneling | 243 |
| Dog and Cat Food | 241 |
| Dry Cell Batteries | 403 |
| Extension Ladders | 418 |
| Fallout Shelters | 229 |
| Feather and Down Products | 253 |
| Fiber Glass Curtains | 413 |
| Food (Games of Chance) | 419 |
| Funerals | 453 |
| Gasoline (Octane posting) | 306 |
| Gasoline | 419 |
| Greeting Cards | 244 |
| Home Entertainment Amplifiers | 432 |
| Home Insulation | 460 |
| Hosiery | 22 |
| Household Furniture | 250 |
| Jewelry | 23 |
| Ladies' Handbags | 247 |
| Law Books | 256 |
| Light Bulbs | 409 |
| Luggage and Related Products | 24 |
| Mail Order Insurance | 234 |
| Mail Order Merchandise | 435 |
| Men's and Boys' Tailored Clothing | 412 |
| Metallic Watch Band | 19 |
| Mirrors | 21 |
| Nursery | 18 |
| Ophthalmic Practices | 456 |
| Photographic Film and Film Processing | 242 |
| Private Vocational and Home Study Schools | 254 |
| Radiation Monitoring Instruments | 232 |
| Retail Food Stores (Advertising) | 424 |
| Shell Homes | 230 |
| Shoes | 231 |
| Sleeping Bags | 400 |
| Tablecloths and Related Products | 404 |
| Television Sets | 410 |
| Textile Wearing Apparel | 423 |

| <u>Industry</u> | <u>Part</u> |
|---|---|
| Textiles | 236 |
| Tires | 228 |
| Used Automobile Parts | 20 |
| Used Lubricating Oil | 406 |
| Used Motor Vehicles | 455 |
| Waist Belts | 405 |
| Watches | 245 |
| Wigs and Hairpieces | 252 |

Some other federal laws that affect businesses are as follows:

✪ *Alcohol Administration Act*

✪ *Child Protection and Toy Safety Act (1969)*

✪ *Clean Water Act*

✪ *Comprehensive Smokeless Tobacco Health Education Act (1986)*

✪ *Consumer Credit Protection Act (1968)*

✪ *Consumer Product Safety Act (1972)*

✪ *Energy Policy and Conservation Act*

✪ *Environmental Pesticide Control Act of 1972*

✪ *Fair Credit Reporting Act (1970)*

✪ *Fair Packaging and Labeling Act (1966)*

✪ *Flammable Fabrics Act (1953)*

✪ *Food, Drug, and Cosmetic Act*

✪ *Fur Products Labeling Act (1951)*

✪ *Hazardous Substances Act (1960)*

✪   *Hobby Protection Act*

✪   *Insecticide, Fungicide, and Rodenticide Act*

✪   *Magnuson-Moss Warranty Act*

✪   *Poison Prevention Packaging Act of 1970*

✪   *Solid Waste Disposal Act*

✪   *Textile Fiber Products Identification Act*

✪   *Toxic Substance Control Act*

✪   *Wool Products Labeling Act (1939)*

✪   *Nutrition Labeling and Education Act of 1990*

✪   *Food Safety Enforcement Enhancement Act of 1997*

# Massachusetts Laws

Massachusetts has numerous laws regulating specific types of businesses or certain activities of businesses. The following is a list of those laws that are most likely to affect small businesses. If you are running a type of business that is not mentioned here, or using some sales technique that could come under government regulation, check the indexes to the Massachusetts General Laws and the Massachusetts Code of Regulations. Since these indexes are not well done, you should look up every possible synonym or related word to be sure not to miss anything. You can find the laws online at **www.state.ma.us/legis/laws/mgl/index.htm** (not an official version, but fairly accurate nonetheless).

Citations refer to Massachusetts General Laws (Mass. Gen. Laws). If no sections are cited, the entire chapter cited applies.

| | Chapter(s) | Section(s) |
|---|---|---|
| Acupuncturists | 112 | 148-162 |
| Adoption Agencies | 210 | |
| Adulteration and misbranding of food and drugs | 94 | 185-196 |
| Agents, consignees and factors | 104 | |
| Agricultural and other seeds | 128 | 84-101 |
| Alcoholic liquors | 138 | |
| Allied mental health and human services professionals | 112 | 163-172 |
| Ambulances and EMTs | 111C | |
| Anti-freeze solutions | 94 | 303G-303M |
| Antitrust act | 93 | |
| Apples | 94 | 100-105 |
| | 128 | 102-115 |
| Architects | 112 | 60A-60O |
| Assignment of wages | 154 | |
| Athletic trainers | 112 | 23F |
| Auctioneers | 100 | |
| Audiologists | 112 | 138-147 |
| Bakeries and bakery products | 94 | 2-10 |
| Baking powder | 94 | 2-10 |
| Bank deposits and collections | 106 | 4-101-4-504 |
| Barbers | 112 | 87F-87S |
| Bells, whistles and gongs | 149 | 175 |
| Brokers | 112 | 87UU |
| Butter, cheese and lard | 94 | 49-63 |
| Cancelation of agreements | 93 | 48-48A |
| Canned goods and molasses | 94 | 154-156 |
| Carriers of property by motor vehicle | 159B | |
| Cemeteries | 114 | |
| Certain business corporations | 156D *(As of July 1, 2004)* | |
| Certified health officers | 112 | 87WWW-87ZZZ |
| Certified public accountants | 112 | 87A-87E ½ |
| Chiropractors | 112 | 89-97 |
| Cinematographers operating in public buildings | 143 | 75 |
| Clinical laboratories | 111D | |
| Coal, coke, charcoal and kindling wood | 94 | 238-249F |
| Cold storage | 94 | 66-73 |
| Collection agencies | 93 | 24-28 |
| Commercial drivers | 90F | |

| | Chapter(s) | Section(s) |
|---|---|---|
| Furs | 94 | 277A |
| Gasoline dealers | 93E | 1-9 |
| Grain and meal | 94 | 219-224 |
| Hay | 94 | 236 |
| Hazardous substances | 94B | |
| Hazardous substances disclosure by employers | 111F | |
| Hazardous waste site cleanup professionals | 21A | 19C |
| Health and safety | 149 | 106-142 |
| Health clubs | 93 | 78-88 |
| Hearing aids | 93 | 71-75 |
| Heating oils | 94 | 249H |
| Herring, alewives, etc. | 130 | 93-96 |
| Home improvement contractors | 142A | |
| Horse and dog racing meetings | 128A | |
| Hospitals, clinics and dispensaries | 111 | 50-57D |
| Ice | 94 | 157-162 |
| Imported goods | 94 | 277B |
| Inland fisheries and game | 131 | |
| Inspection and sale of meat | 94 | 146-153A |
| Insurance agents | 175 | |
| Insurance premium finance agencies | 255C | |
| Junkyards | 140B | |
| Kennel operators | 140 | 137A |
| Kosher foods | 94 | 156 |
| Labels, trademarks and trade names | 110 | |
| Land surveyors | 112 | 81D-81T |
| Landscape architects | 112 | 98-107 |
| Laundries and dry cleaning establishments | 93 | 18A, 18B |
| Liability of employers to employees for injuries not resulting in a death | 153 | |
| Lime and lime casks | 94 | 262-268 |
| Limited partnerships | 109 | |
| Lobsters | 130 | 37-51A |
| Manufacturers and sellers of upholstered furniture, bedding, or stuffed toys or filling for same | 94 | 271 |
| Maple syrup and maple syrup food products | 128 | 36C |
| Marine fish and fisheries | 130 | |
| Marking of packages containing food | 94 | 181-184E |

| | Chapter(s) | Section(s) |
|---|---|---|
| Physicians and surgeons | 112 | 2-9B, 10-12CC |
| Physicians assistants | 112 | 9C-9K |
| Pick-your-own farming operations | 128 | 2E |
| Pilots | 103 | |
| Plant closings | 151A | 71A-71H |
| Plumbers | 142 | |
| Podiatrists | 112 | 13-22 |
| Potatoes | 94 | 117G-117L |
| Professional corporations | 156A | |
| Prohibition of certain discrimination by businesses | 151E | |
| Psychologists | 112 | 118-137 |
| Public warehouses | 105 | |
| Radio and television technicians | 112 | 87PPP-87VVV |
| Real estate brokers and salesmen | 112 | 87PP-87DDD½ |
| Real estate appraisers | 112 | 173-195 |
| Registration and protection of trademarks | 110B | |
| Regulation of business practices for consumers protection | 93A | 1-11 |
| Removal, termination or fire sales | 93 | 28A-28F |
| Rental agreements for personal property used primarily for household or family use | 93 | 90-94 |
| Research institutions using dogs or cats for experimentation | 140 | 174D |
| Respiratory therapists | 112 | 23R-23BB |
| Retail clothing stores dressing room surveillance | 93 | 89 |
| Retail drug stores | 112 | 37-42A |
| Retail trade reporting agencies | 93 | 49A |
| Sales | 106 | 2-101--2-725 |
| Sales by weight | 94 | 176-180 |
| Sales financiers | 255B | 2 |
| Sanitarians | 112 | 87LL-87OO |
| Sausages | 94 | 142-143A |
| Scallops | 130 | 92 |
| School bus operators | 90 | 8-8A 1/2 |
| Secured transactions | 106 | 9-101--9-507 |
| Self-service storage facilities | 105A | |
| Sellers of ammunitions | 140 | 122B |
| Sellers of milk or cream to other than consumers | 94 | 41A |
| Shellfish | 130 | 52-75 |

If you want to stay with the traditional dot-com ending, it may seem like most words have been taken as a dot-com name. However, if you combine two or three short words or abbreviations, a nearly unlimited number of possibilities are available. For example, if you have a business dealing with automobiles, most likely someone has already registered automobile.com and auto.com. But you can come up with all kinds of variations, using adjectives or your name, depending on your type of business. For example, you could come up with:

| | | |
|---|---|---|
| autos4u.com | joesauto.com | autobob.com |
| myauto.com | yourauto.com | onlyautos.com |
| greatauto.com | autosfirst.com | usautos.com |
| greatautos.com | firstautoworld.com | 4autos.com |

One site that provides both low cost registrations and suggestions for name variations is **www.registerfly.com**.

When the Internet first began, some individuals realized that major corporations would soon want to register their names. Since the registration was easy and cheap, people registered names they thought would ultimately be used by someone else.

At first, some companies paid high fees to buy their names from the registrants. But one company, Intermatic, filed a lawsuit instead of paying. The owner of the mark they wanted had registered numerous trademarks, such as britishairways.com and ussteel.com. The court ruled that since Intermatic owned a trademark on the name, the registration of their name by someone else violated that trademark and that Intermatic was entitled to it.

Since then people have registered names that are not trademarks, such as CalRipkin.com, and have attempted to charge the individuals with those names to buy their domain. In 1998, Congress stepped in and passed the *Anti-Cybersquatting Consumer Protection Act*. This law makes it illegal to register a domain with no legitimate need to use it.

This law helped a lot of companies protect their names, but then some companies started abusing it and tried to stop legitimate users of similar names. This is especially likely against small companies. An organization that has been set up to help small companies protect their domains is the Domain Name Rights Coalition. Its website is **www.domainnamerights.org**.

Registering a domain name for your own business is a simple process. There are many companies that offer registration services. For a list of those companies, visit the site of the Internet Corporation for Assigned Names and Numbers (ICANN) at **www.icann.org**. You can link directly to any member's site and compare the costs and registration procedures required for the different top-level domains.

# Web Pages

There are many new companies eager to help you set up a website. Some offer turnkey sites for a low flat rate. Custom sites can cost tens of thousands of dollars. If you have plenty of capital you may want to have your site handled by one of these professionals. However, setting up a website is a fairly simple process. Once you learn the basics, you can handle most of it in-house.

If you are new to the Web, you may want to look at **www.learnthenet.com** and **www.webopedia.com**. They will familiarize you with the Internet jargon and give you a basic introduction to the Web.

*Site Set-Up*    There are seven steps to setting up a website: site purpose, design, content, structure, programming, testing, and publicity. Whether you do it yourself, hire a professional site designer, or use a college student, the steps toward creating an effective site are the same.

Before beginning your own site you should look at other sites, including those of major corporations and of small businesses. Look at the sites of all the companies that compete with you. Look at hundreds of sites and click through them to see how they work (or do not work).

*Site purpose.* To know what to include on your site you must decide what its purpose will be. Do you want to take orders for your products or services, attract new employees, give away samples, or show off your company headquarters? You might want to do several of these things.

*Site design.* After looking at other sites you can see that there are numerous ways to design a site. It can be crowded or open and airy. It can have several windows (frames) open at once or just one. It can allow long scrolling or just click-throughs.

You will have to decide whether the site will have text only; text plus photographs and graphics; or text plus photos, graphics, and other design elements such as animation or Java script. Additionally, you will begin to make decisions about colors, fonts, and the basic graphic appearance of the site.

*Site content.* You must create the content for your site. For this, you can use your existing promotional materials, you can write new material just for the website, or you can use a combination of the two. Whatever you choose, remember that the written material should be concise, free of errors, and easy for your target audience to read. Any graphics, including photographs and written materials, not created by you require permission. You should obtain such permission from the lawful copyright holder in order to use any copyrighted material. Once you know your site's purpose, look, and content, you can begin to piece the site together.

*Site structure.* You must decide how the content (text plus photographs, graphics, animation, etc.) will be structured—what content will be on which page, and how a user will link from one part of the site to another. For example, your first page may have the business name and then choices to click on, such as *about us*, *opportunities*, *product catalog*, etc. Have those choices connect to another page containing the detailed information so that a user will see the catalog when they click on *product catalog*. Or your site could have a choice to click on a link to another website related to yours.

*Site programming and setup.* When you know nothing about setting up a website, it can seem like a daunting task that will require an expert. However, *programming* here means merely putting a site together. There are inexpensive computer programs available that make it very simple.

Commercial programs such as *Microsoft FrontPage*, *Dreamweaver*, *Pagemaker*, *Photoshop*, *MS Publisher*, and *PageMill* allow you to set up Web pages as easily as laying out a print publication. These programs will convert the text and graphics you create into HTML, the programming language of the Web. Before you choose Web design software and design your site, you should determine which Web hosting service you will use. Make sure that the design software you use is compatible with the host server's system. The Web host will be the provider who will give you space on their server and who may provide other services to you, such as secure order processing and analysis of your site to see who is visiting and linking to it.

If you have an America Online account, you can download design software and a tutorial for free. You do not have to use AOL's design software in order to use this service. You are eligible to use this site whether you design your own pages, have someone else do the design work for you, or use AOL's templates. This service allows you to use your own domain name and choose the package that is appropriate for your business.

If you have used a page layout program, you can usually get a simple Web page up and running within a day or two. If you do not have much experience with a computer, you might consider hiring a college student to set up a Web page for you.

*Site testing.* Some of the website setup programs allow you to thoroughly check your new site to see if all the pictures are included and all the links are proper. There are also websites you can go to that will check out your site. Some even allow you to improve your site, such as by reducing the size of your graphics so they download faster. Use a major search engine listed on page 140 to look for companies that can test your site before you launch it on the Web.

*Site publicity.* Once you set up your website, you will want to get people to look at it. *Publicity* means getting your site noticed as much as possible by drawing people to it.

The first thing to do to get noticed is to be sure your site is registered with as many *search engines* as possible. These are pages that people use to find things on the Internet, such as Yahoo and Excite. They do not automatically know about you just because you created a website. You must tell them about your site. They then examine and catalog it.

For a fee, there are services that will register your site with numerous search engines. If you are starting out on a shoestring, you can easily do it yourself. While there are hundreds of search engines, most people use a dozen or so of the bigger ones. If your site is in a niche area, such as genealogy services, then you would want to be listed on any specific genealogy search engines. Most businesses should be mainly concerned with getting on the biggest ones.

If your site gets enough viewers, people may pay you to place their ads there. Another possibility is to trade ads with another site. In fact there are companies that broker ad trades among websites.

**NOTE:** *Such trades used to be taxable transactions, but after January 5, 2000, such trades were no longer taxable under IRS Notice 2000-6.*

# Legal Issues

Before you set up a Web page, you should consider some important legal issues.

***Jurisdiction***   Jurisdiction is the power of a court in a particular location to decide a particular case. Usually you have to have been physically present in a jurisdiction or have done business there before you can be sued there. Since the Internet extends your business's ability to reach people in faraway places, there may be instances when you could be subject to legal jurisdiction far from your own state (or country). There are a number of cases that have been decided in this country regarding the Internet and jurisdiction, but very few cases have been decided on this issue outside of the United States.

In most instances, U.S. courts use the pre-Internet test–whether you have been present in another jurisdiction or have had enough contact with someone in the other jurisdiction. The fact that the Internet itself is not a *place* will not shield you from being sued in another state when you have shipped you company's product there, have entered into a contract with a resident of that state, or have defamed a foreign resident with content on your website.

According to one court, there is a spectrum of contact required between you, your website, and consumers. (*Zippo Manufacturing Co. v. Zippo Dot Com, Inc.,* 952 F. Supp. 1119 (W.D. Pa 1997)) It is clear that the one end of the spectrum includes the shipping, contracting, and defamation mentioned as sufficient to establish jurisdiction. The more interactive your site is with consumers, the more you target an audience for your goods in a particular location, and the farther you reach to send your goods out into the world, the more it becomes possible for someone to sue you outside of your own jurisdiction—possibly even in another country.

The law is not even remotely final on these issues. The American Bar Association, among other groups, is studying this topic in detail. At present, no final, global solution or agreement about jurisdictional issues exists.

One way to protect yourself from the possibility of being sued in a faraway jurisdiction would be to have a statement on your website stating that those using the site or doing business with you agree that *jurisdiction for any actions regarding this site* or your company will be in your home county.

For extra protection you can have a preliminary page that must be clicked before entering your website. However, this may be overkill for a small business with little risk of lawsuits. If you are in any business for which you could have serious liability, you should review some competitors' sites and see how they handle the liability issue. They often have a place to click for *legal notice* or *disclaimer* on their first page.

You may want to consult with an attorney to discuss the specific disclaimer you will use on your website, where it should appear, and whether you will have users of your site actively *agree* to this disclaimer or just *passively* read it. However, these disclaimers are not enforceable everywhere in the world. Until there is global agreement on jurisdictional issues, this may remain an area of uncertainty for some time to come.

**Libel**

*Libel* is any publication that injures the reputation of another. This can occur in print, writing, pictures, or signs. All that is required for *publication* is that you transmit the material to at least one other person. When putting together your website you must keep in mind that it is visible to millions of people all over the planet and that if you libel a person or company you may have to pay damages. Many countries do not have the freedom of speech that we do and a statement that is not libel in the United States may be libelous elsewhere.

**Copyright Infringement**

It is so easy to copy and *borrow* information on the Internet that it is easy to infringe copyrights without even knowing it. A *copyright* exists for a work as soon as the creator creates it. There is no need to register the copyright or to put a copyright notice on it. So, practically everything on the Internet belongs to someone. Some people freely give their works away. For example, many people have created web artwork (*gifs* and *animated gifs*) that they freely allow people to copy.

There are numerous sites that provide hundreds or thousands of free gifs that you can add to your Web pages. Some require you to acknowledge the source; some do not. You should always be sure that the works are free for the taking before using them.

**Linking and Framing**     One way to violate copyright laws is to improperly link other sites to yours either directly or with framing. *Linking* is when you provide a place on your site to click that takes someone to another site. *Framing* occurs when you set up your site so that when you link to another site, your site is still viewable as a frame around the linked-to site.

While many sites are glad to be linked to others, some, especially providers of valuable information, object. Courts have ruled that linking and framing can be a copyright violation. One rule that has developed is that it is usually okay to link to the first page of a site, but not to link to some valuable information deeper within the site. The rationale for this is that the owner of the site wants visitors to go through the various levels of their site (viewing all the ads) before getting the information. By linking to the information you are giving away their product without the ads.

The problem with linking to the first page of a site is that it may be a tedious or difficult task to find the needed page from there. Many sites are poorly designed and make it nearly impossible to find anything.

The best solution, if you wish to link to another page, is to ask permission. Email the Webmaster or other person in charge of the site, if one is given, and explain what you want to do. If they grant permission, be sure to print out a copy of their email for your records.

**Privacy**     Since the Internet is such an easy way to share information, there are many concerns that it will cause a loss of individual privacy. The two main concerns arise when you post information that others consider private, and when you gather information from customers and use it in a way that violates their privacy.

While public actions of politicians and celebrities are fair game, details about their private lives are sometimes protected by law. Details about persons who are not public figures are often protected. The laws in each state are different and what might be allowable in one state could be illegal in another. If your site will provide any personal information about individuals, discuss the possibility of liability with an attorney.

Several well-known companies have been in the news lately for violations of their customers' privacy. They either shared what the customer was buying or downloading or looked for additional information on the customer's computer. To let customers know that you do not violate certain standards of privacy, you can subscribe to one of the privacy codes that have been promulgated for the Internet. These allow you to put a symbol on your site guaranteeing to your customers that you follow the code.

The websites of two organizations that offer this service, and their fees at the time of this publication, are:

www.privacybot.com    $100
www.bbbonline.com    $200 to $7,000

**Protecting Yourself**

The easiest way to protect yourself personally from the various possible types of liability is to set up a corporation or limited liability company to own the website. This is not foolproof protection since, in some cases, you could be sued personally as well, but it is one level of protection.

**COPPA**

If your website is aimed at children under the age of thirteen, or if it attracts children of that age, then you are subject to the federal *Children Online Privacy Protection Act of 1998* (COPPA). This law requires such websites to:

✪ give notice on the site of what information is being collected;

✪ obtain verifiable parental consent to collect the information;

✪ allow the parent to review the information collected;

✪ allow the parent to delete the child's information or to refuse to allow the use of the information;

✪ limit the information collected to only that necessary to participate on the site; and,

✪ protect the security and confidentiality of the information.

✪    *What's Dot and What's Not: Domain Name Registration Scams*

✪    *You, Your Privacy Policy & COPPA*

These publications are available from the FTC website at **www.ftc.gov/bcp/ menu-internet.htm** or by mail from:

**Consumer Response Center**
Federal Trade Commission
600 Pennsylvania, NW
Room H-130
Washington, DC 20580-0001

# Fraud

Because the Internet is somewhat anonymous, it is a tempting place for those with fraudulent schemes to look for victims. As a business consumer, you should exercise caution when dealing with unknown or anonymous parties on the Internet.

The U.S. Department of Justice, the FBI, and the National White Collar Crime Center jointly launched the Internet Fraud Complaint Center (IFCC). If you suspect that you are the victim of fraud online, whether as a consumer or a business, you can report incidents to the IFCC on their website, **www.ifccfbi.gov**. The IFCC is currently staffed by FBI agents and representatives of the National White Collar Crime Center and will work with state and local law enforcement officials to prevent, investigate, and prosecute high-tech and economic crime online.

# 16 BOOKKEEPING AND ACCOUNTING

It is beyond the scope of this book to explain all the intricacies of setting up a business' bookkeeping and accounting systems. But the important thing to realize is that if you do not set up an understandable bookkeeping system, your business will undoubtedly fail.

Without accurate records of where your income is coming from and where it is going, you will be unable to increase your profits, lower your expenses, obtain needed financing, or make the right decisions in all areas of your business. The time to decide how you will handle your bookkeeping is when you open your business, not a year later when it is tax time.

## Initial Bookkeeping

If you do not understand business taxation, you should pick up a good book on the subject, as well as the IRS tax guide for your type of business (proprietorship, partnership, or corporation).

The IRS tax book for small businesses is Publication 334, *Tax Guide for Small Businesses*. There are also instruction booklets for each type of business form:

Schedule C for proprietorships, Form 1120 or 1120S for C corporations and S corporations, and 1165 for partnerships and businesses that are taxed like partnerships (LLCs, LLPs).

Keep in mind that the IRS does not give you the best advice for saving on taxes and does not give you the other side of contested issues. You need a private tax guide or advisor for that.

The most important thing to do is to set up your bookkeeping so that you can easily fill out your monthly, quarterly, and annual tax returns. The best way to do this is to get copies of the returns, note the categories that you will need to supply, and set up your bookkeeping system to arrive at those totals. For example, for a sole proprietorship you will use *Schedule C* to report business income and expenses to the IRS at the end of the year. Use the categories on that form to sort your expenses. To make your job especially easy, every time you pay a bill, put the category number on the check.

# Accountants

Your new business will most likely not be able to afford hiring an accountant right off to handle your books. That is good. Doing your own bookkeeping and tax preparation will force you to learn about business accounting and taxation. The worst way to run a business is to know nothing about the tax laws and turn everything over to an accountant at the end of the year to find out what is due.

You should know the basics of tax law before making basic decisions such as whether to buy or rent equipment or premises. You should understand accounting so you can time your financial affairs appropriately. If your business needs to buy supplies, inventory, or equipment and provides goods or services throughout the year, you need to at least have a basic understanding of the system within which you are working.

Once you can afford an accountant, you should weigh the cost against your time and the risk that you will make an error. Even if you think you know enough to do your own corporate tax return, you should still take it to an accountant one year to see if you have been missing any deductions. You might decide that the money saved is worth the cost of the accountant's services.

# Computer Programs

Today, every business should keep its books by computer. There are inexpensive programs such as Quicken that can instantly provide you with reports of your income and expenses and the right figures to plug into your tax returns.

Most programs even offer a tax program each year that will take all of your information and print it out on the current year's tax forms.

# Tax Tips

Using these tax tips for small businesses can help you save money.

- ✪ Usually when you buy equipment for a business, you must amortize the cost over several years. That is, you do not deduct it all when you buy it, you take, say, twenty-five percent of the cost off your taxes each year for four years. (The time is determined by the theoretical usefulness of the item.) However, small businesses are allowed to write off the entire cost of a limited amount of items under Internal Revenue Code, Section 179. If you have income to shelter, use it.

- ✪ Owners of S corporations do not have to pay Social Security or Medicare taxes on the part of their profits that is not considered salary. As long as you pay yourself a reasonable salary, other money you take out is not subject to these taxes.

- ✪ You should not neglect to deposit withholding taxes for your own salary or profits. Besides being a large sum to come up with at once in April, there are penalties that must be paid for failure to do so.

- ✪ Do not fail to keep track of and remit your employees' withholding. You will be personally liable for them even if you are a corporation.

- ✪ If you keep track of the use of your car for business, you can deduct mileage. (The amount can go up or down each year.) You may be able to depreciate your car if you use it for business for a considerable amount of time.

ter, IRS Form ES-1040 must be filed by each partner along with payment of one-quarter of the amount of income tax and Social Security taxes estimated to be due for the year.

**C Corporation**

A regular corporation is a separate taxpayer and pays tax on its profits after deducting all expenses, including officers' salaries. If dividends are distributed, they are paid out of after-tax dollars, and the shareholders pay tax a second time on the dividends they receive. If a corporation needs to accumulate money for investment, it may be able to do so at lower tax rates than the shareholders. But if all profits will be distributed to shareholders, the double-taxation may be excessive unless all income is paid as salaries. C corporations file IRS Form 1120.

**S Corporation**

A small corporation has the option of being taxed like a partnership. If IRS Form 2553 is filed by the corporation and accepted by the Internal Revenue Service, the S corporation will only file an informational return listing profits and expenses. Each shareholder will be taxed on a proportional share of the profits (or be able to deduct a proportional share of the losses). Unless a corporation will make a large profit that will not be distributed, S-status is usually best in the beginning. An S corporation files IRS Form 1120S and distributes IRS Form K-1 to each shareholder. If any money is taken out by a shareholder that is not listed as wages subject to withholding, then the shareholder will usually have to file IRS Form ES-1040 each quarter along with payment of the estimated withholding on the withdrawals.

**Limited Liability Companies and Partnerships**

Limited liability companies and limited liability partnerships are allowed by the IRS to elect to be taxed either as a partnership or a corporation. LLCs that elect to be taxed as corporations can also elect to be taxed as S corporations. To make this election, you file IRS Form 8832, *Entity Classification Election*, with the IRS. However, you need not file IRS Form 8832 if you wish to be treated under the *default rules*. These rules provide, among other things, that a *domestic eligible entity* will be treated as a partnership if it has two or more members.

**Tax Workshops and Booklets**

The IRS conducts workshops to inform businesses about the tax laws. (Do not expect in-depth study of the loopholes.) For information about any of these programs, contact the Taxpayer Education Coordinator at:

JFK Federal Building
Stop 40726
15 New Sudbury St.
Boston, MA 02203-9112
800-829-1040
617-565-4325 (Boston only)

# Federal Withholding, Social Security, and Medicare Taxes

If you need basic information on business tax returns, the IRS publishes a rather large booklet that answers most questions and is available free of charge. Call or write them and ask for Publication No. 334. If you have any questions, look up their toll-free number in the phone book under United States Government/Internal Revenue Service. If you want more creative answers and tax saving information, find a good local accountant. But to get started, you will need the following.

**Employer Identification Number**

If you are a sole proprietor with no employees, you can use your Social Security number for your business. If you are a corporation, a partnership, or a proprietorship with employees, you must obtain an *Employer Identification Number*. This is done by filing an **APPLICATION FOR EMPLOYER IDENTIFICATION NUMBER (IRS FORM SS-4)** (form 5, p.199). It usually takes a week or two to receive. You will need this number to open bank accounts for the business, so you should file this form a soon as you decide to go into business. A sample filled-in form and instructions are included in Appendix A.

**Employee's Withholding Allowance Certificate**

You must have each employee fill out an **EMPLOYEES WITHHOLDING ALLOWANCE CERTIFICATE (IRS FORM W-4)** (form 7, p.213) to calculate the amount of federal taxes to be deducted and to obtain their social security numbers. (The number of allowances on this form is used with IRS Circular E, Publication 15, to figure out the exact deductions.) A sample filled-in form is included in Appendix A.

**Federal Tax Deposit Coupons**

After taking withholdings from employees' wages, you must deposit them at a bank that is authorized to accept such funds. If at the end of any month you have over $1,000 in withheld taxes (including your contribution to FICA) you must make a deposit prior to the 15th of the following month. If on the 3rd, 7th, 11th, 15th, 19th, 22nd, or 25th of any month you have over $3,000 in withheld taxes, you must make a deposit within three banking days. The deposit is made using the coupons in the IRS Form 8109 booklet.

Businesses that make $50,000 or more a year in federal tax deposits are required to use electronic filing.

**Estimated Tax Payment Voucher**

Sole proprietors and partners usually take draws from their businesses without the formality of withholding. However, they are still required to make deposits of income and FICA taxes each quarter. If more than $500 is due in April on a person's 1040 form, then not enough money was withheld each quarter and a penalty is assessed unless the person falls into an exception. The quarterly withholding is submitted on IRS Form 1040-ES on April 15th, June 15th, September 15th, and January 15th each year. If these days fall on a weekend then the due date is the following Monday. The worksheet with IRS Form 1040-ES can be used to determine the amount to pay.

NOTE: *One of the exceptions to the rule is that if you withhold the same amount as last year's tax bill, then you do not have to pay a penalty. This is usually a lot easier than filling out the IRS Form 1040-ES worksheet.*

**Employer's Quarterly Tax Return**

Each quarter you must file IRS Form 941 reporting your federal withholding and FICA taxes. If you owe more than $1,000 at the end of a quarter, you are required to make a deposit at the end of any month that you have $1,000 in withholding. The deposits are made to the Federal Reserve Bank or an authorized financial institution on Form 501. Most banks are authorized to accept deposits. If you owe more than $3,000 for any month, you must make a deposit at any point in the month in which you owe $3,000. After you file **IRS FORM SS-4**, the 941 forms will be sent to you automatically if you checked the box saying that you expect to have employees.

**Wage and Tax Statement**

At the end of each year, you are required to issue an IRS Form W-2 to each employee. This form shows the amount of wages paid to the employee during the year as well as the amounts withheld for taxes, Social Security, Medicare, and other purposes.

If you pay at least $600 to a person other than an employee (such as independent contractors), you are required to file an IRS Form 1099 for that person. Along with the 1099s, you must file an IRS Form 1096, which is a summary sheet.

Many people are not aware of this law and fail to file these forms. They are required for such things as services, royalties, rents, awards, and prizes that you pay to individuals (but not corporations). The rules for this are quite complicated so you should either obtain *Package 1099* from the IRS or consult your accountant.

**Earned Income Credit**

Persons who are not liable to pay income tax may have the right to a check from the government because of the *Earned Income Credit*. You are required to notify your employees of this. You can satisfy this requirement with one of the following:

✪   a W-2 Form with the notice on the back;

✪   a substitute for the W-2 Form with the notice on it;

✪   a copy of Notice 797; or,

✪   a written statement with the wording from Notice 797.

A Notice 797 can be obtained by calling 800-829-3676.

# Federal Excise Taxes

Excise taxes are taxes on certain activities or items. Most federal excise taxes have been eliminated since World War II, but a few still remain.

Some of the things that are subject to federal excise taxes are tobacco and alcohol, gasoline, tires and inner tubes, some trucks and trailers, firearms, ammunition, bows, arrows, fishing equipment, the use of highway vehicles of over 55,000 pounds, aircraft, wagering, telephone and teletype services, coal, hazardous wastes, and vaccines. If you are involved with any of these, you should obtain from the IRS publication No. 510, *Information on Excise Taxes.*

# Federal Unemployment Compensation Taxes

You must pay federal unemployment taxes if you paid wages of $1,500 in any quarter or if you had at least one employee for twenty calendar weeks. The federal tax amount is 0.8% of the first $7,000 of wages paid each employee. If more than $100 is due by the end of any quarter (if you paid $12,500 in wages for the quarter), then IRS Form 508 must be filed with an authorized financial institution or the Federal Reserve Bank in your area. You will receive IRS Form 508 when you obtain your employer identification number.

At the end of each year, you must file IRS Form 940 or IRS Form 940EZ. This is your annual report of federal unemployment taxes. You will receive an original form from the IRS.

# 18 | PAYING MASSACHUSETTS TAXES

In addition to federal taxes, the Commonwealth of Massachusetts imposes certain taxes of its own.

## Sales and Use Tax

If you will be selling or renting goods or services at retail, you must collect Massachusetts Sales and Use Tax. The sales and use tax rate is 5%. Certain items are exempt from sales tax, such as clothing items under $175 and food not bought for immediate consumption. Some services, such as doctors' and lawyers' services and newspaper advertising, are not taxed, but most others are.

The sales tax also applies to meals (it is also called the *Meals Tax*). *Meals* for this purpose is defined as any food or beverage that has been prepared for immediate consumption, including take-out. The meals tax return is similar to the sales tax return. Returns are due monthly.

First, you must obtain a tax number by filling out an Application for Original Registration (TA-1) and paying a small fee. Form TA-1 can no longer be filed on paper. It must be filed online at **www.massdor.com/options/TA1/ta1_home.htm**. For more details about the tax, see **www.massdor.com/options/TA1/instruct.htm**. You can obtain the form by calling 800-392-6089.

If your sales and use tax liability (excluding meals tax) is reasonably expected to be over $1,200 for the year, you must file monthly returns and pay the taxes due for each month by the twentieth day of the next month. If your liability is under $100, you can file and pay annually; and if between $100 and $1,200, you can file and pay quarterly.

Once you file your Form TA-1, you will have to start filing returns whether you have any sales or not. A sample **MONTHLY SALES TAX RETURN (ST-9)** is provided in Appendix A and a blank form is contained in Appendix B. (see form 8, p.215.)

One reason to get a tax number early is to exempt your purchases from tax. When you buy a product that you will resell, or use as part of a product that you will sell, you are exempt from paying tax on it. You need to submit a *Resale Certificate* to the seller to get the exemption. This form must contain your sales and use tax registration number.

If you will only be selling items wholesale or out of state, you might think that you do not need a tax number or to submit returns, but you will need to be registered to obtain the tax number to exempt your purchases.

If you have any sales before you get your monthly tax return forms, you should calculate the tax anyway and submit it. Otherwise, you will be charged a penalty regardless of whether or not it was your fault that you did not have the forms.

After you obtain your tax number, you will be required to collect sales tax on all purchases.

If you sell to someone who claims to be exempt from sales and use taxes, (for example, if they plan to resell merchandise they have purchased from you) then they must present to you the previously mentioned Resale Certificate.

**Income Tax Withholding**

All employers are required to withhold a portion of their employees' wages for state income tax purposes. If the withheld amount is less than $100 annually the return is due annually. If the withheld amount is between $101 and $1200 annually, the return is due quarterly. If the amount withheld is between $1201 and $25,000 annually, the return is due monthly. If the withheld amount is over $25,000 annually, the return periods vary but can be required weekly. A sample **EMPLOYER'S MONTHLY RETURN OF INCOME TAX WITHHELD (M-942)** (form 9) is shown on page 184, and a blank form is contained in Appendix B.

***Room Occupancy Tax***

Individuals operating hotels, motels, lodging houses, or private clubs offering sleeping accommodations must pay room occupancy tax of 5.7% on rooms rented for $15 or more per day to persons occupying the rooms for 90 consecutive days or less. Returns are due monthly.

***Cigarette and Tobacco Tax***

The state also imposes taxes on the sale of cigarettes, smoking tobacco, and cigars. Returns are due monthly.

# Corporate Excise (Income) Tax

Massachusetts taxes corporations based on their Massachusetts income and their tangible and intangible property. The minimum tax (even for S corporations) is $456 per year. Estimated tax payments must be made during the year if your liability will be over $1,000 for the year.

The corporate income tax rate is 9.5% on income attributable to Massachusetts. Contact the Massachusetts Department of Revenue for more information.

# Unemployment Compensation Taxes

You are not liable to pay unemployment compensation taxes until you have had an employee work a part of a day in any thirteen calendar weeks or paid $1,500 in wages in a quarter. But once you reach that point, you are liable for all back taxes. The rate varies according to your employment record. The tax is paid on the first $10,800 of wages of each employee.

If you anticipate having an employee for thirteen weeks or when you have had an employee work for thirteen weeks, you should file an **EMPLOYER'S STATUS REPORT (FORM 1110-A)** (form 10, p.219). A sample filled-in **FORM 1110-A** may be found on page 185. You will be sent quarterly returns to complete.

The Department of Revenue's website at **www.dor.state.ma.us** has a wealth of information, instructions, and forms to assist the business owner in complying with the state's tax requirements. Many of the returns can be filed electronically. See a list of online state tax forms at **www.dor.state.ma.us/forms/formlist.htm**.

# 19 Out-of-State Taxes

At present, companies are only required to collect sales taxes for states in which they *do business*. Exactly what business is enough to trigger taxation is a legal question and some states try to define it as broadly as possible.

If you have an office in a state, you are doing business there, and any goods shipped to consumers in that state are subject to sales taxes. If you have a full time employee working in the state most of the year, many states will consider you doing business there. In some states, attending a two-day trade show is enough business to trigger taxation for the entire year for every order shipped to the state.

**NOTE:** *One loophole that often works is to be represented at shows by persons who are not your employees.*

Because the laws are different in each state, you will have to do some research on a state-by-state basis to find out how much business you can do in a state without being subject to their taxation. You can request a state's rules from its department of revenue, but keep in mind that what a department of revenue wants the law to be is not always what the courts will rule that it is.

# Business Taxes

Being subject to a state's income or other business taxes is even worse than being bound to a state's sales taxes. For example, California charges every company doing business in the state a minimum $800 a year fee and charges income tax on a portion of the company's worldwide income. Doing a small amount of business in the state is clearly not worth getting mired in California taxation.

For this reason, some trade shows have been moved from the state and this has resulted in a review of the tax policies and some *safe-harbor* guidelines to advise companies on what they can do without becoming subject to taxation.

Write to the department of revenue of any state with which you have business contacts to see what might trigger your taxation.

# Internet Taxes

State revenue departments are drooling at the prospect of taxing commerce on the Internet. Theories have already been proposed that websites available to state residents mean a company is doing business in a state. Fortunately, Congress has passed a moratorium on taxation of the Internet.

# Canadian Taxes

The Canadian government expects American companies that sell goods by mail order to Canadians, to collect taxes for them and file returns with Revenue Canada, their tax department. Those that receive an occasional unsolicited order are not expected to register, and Canadian customers who order things from the U.S. pay the tax plus a $5 fee upon receipt of the goods. Nonetheless, companies that solicit Canadian orders are expected to be registered if their worldwide income is $30,000 or more per year. In some cases, a company may be required to post a bond and to pay for the cost of Canadian auditors visiting its premises and auditing its books! You may notice that some companies decline to accept orders from Canada for these reasons.

# 20 THE END... AND THE BEGINNING

If you have read through this whole book, you know more about the rules and laws for operating a Massachusetts business than most people in business today. However, after learning about all the governmental regulations, you may become discouraged. You are probably wondering how you can keep track of all the laws and how you will have any time left to make money after complying with the laws. It is not that bad. People are starting businesses every day and they are making money, lots of money.

The regulations that exist right now are enough to strangle some businesses. One way to avoid problems with the government is to keep a low profile and avoid open confrontation. The important thing is that you know the laws and the penalties for violations before making your decision. Knowing the laws will also allow you to use the loopholes in the laws to avoid violations.

# Glossary

## A

**authorized shares.** When a corporation is formed, it is divided into parts called shares. A certain number of shares are authorized by filing organizational documents with the state. The number authorized may be changed later by shareholder vote and amendment to the organizational documents. The corporation may not at any time issue a number of shares greater than the number authorized. The shares issued, also called *outstanding* or *issued and outstanding*, at any point in time comprise the entire ownership of the company. In theory, there could be only one share authorized and issued, owned by one person, which would comprise 100% of the ownership of the company.

More often, the corporation is formed with multiple shares authorized, which can range from a small number (often 275 shares, especially in Massachusetts) to a large number (50,000,000 shares or more). The right number of shares to choose depends on several factors—for example, the number of current owners and potential owners, and the fees charged by each state for authorizing shares. Not all authorized shares need be issued—some, or most, can be reserved for future use (for example, an IPO).

# B

**business certificate.**  A filing that must be made with a town or city clerk by persons and entities doing business under a name other than their true legal name, also called a *trade name* or *fictitious name.*

**buy-sell agreement.**  An agreement among shareholders governing the sale or other transfer of shares. It usually includes what happens if a shareholder working for the corporation leaves the job, is fired, dies, or becomes disabled. Buy-Sell Agreements can also include voting agreements regarding the voting of shares and other corporate governance provisions.

# C

**C corporation.**  One of the types of entities under which you may do business and achieve the protections of limited liability so that only the assets of the entity, not those of its owners, can be used to satisfy liabilities and obligations incurred by that business. C corporations may have unlimited numbers of shareholders. Publicly traded companies are C corporations.

**copyright.**  The legal right granted to an author, composer, playwright, publisher, or distributor to exclusive publication, production, sale, or distribution of a literary, musical, dramatic, or artistic work.  This allows the copyright's owner to (a) prevent a copier from using the copy or copies and (b) compensatory damages under certain conditions.

**corporation.**  A body that is granted a charter recognizing it as a separate legal entity having its own rights, privileges, and liabilities distinct from those of its members. Corporations are entities created by the state in which they are formed. There are no *federal* corporations; each one is registered and created by a state. Once a corporation is established, it may be registered to do business in other states. Doing business through a corporation is one way to protect the owners' personal assets.

# D

**domain name.** A series of letters used to name organizations, computers and addresses on the Internet. Every computer on the Internet has an *address,* which is a series of numbers much like a telephone number. (In technical jargon that address is called the *IP* address. IP stands for Internet Protocol.) The Domain Name System allows the use of more familiar names to reference those computers. There cannot be duplicate names. Each name is linked by the registration system to the unique string of numbers used to identify the computers. Once a name is taken, someone else cannot use it unless the first party relinquishes the name.

# E

**employee.** A worker who is subject to the supervision and control of management with respect to the manner and means of work done.

# F

**fictitious name.** *See business certificate.*

# G

**general partnership.** *See partnership.*

# I

**independent contractor.** A person who works on his or her own, rather than as an employee. If management has the right to supervise and control the manner and means of work done by an individual, that individual is normally called an *employee*. If a worker controls his or her own work methods, works for more than one entity, sets his or her own hours, and provides his or her own equipment, the person will usually be deemed an *independent contractor*. Taxes are collected and paid differently with respect to employees vs. independent contractors.

**initial public offering (IPO).** The first time a corporation offers its stock to the public (*goes public*). This is different from a *private placement*, in which stock or other securities may be offered to a limited number of individuals, or individuals who meet certain criteria.

# L

**limited.** One of the words that many states allow in a corporation's name as an indication that the company is of limited liability status. All states require corporations to use a word such as corporation, incorporated, or limited to indicate to the public that the entity is a limited liability entity.

**limited liability company (LLC).** A legal entity with characteristics of both a corporation and a partnership. The tax treatment of an LLC is similar to that of a partnership—that is, the income is not taxed at the entity level, but at the equity owner level. But the LLC also has the benefit of limited liability, meaning that the owners are not personally liable for the business's debts and obligations. Its limited liability protection is similar to that of a corporation.

**limited liability entity.** An entity whose equity owners are not personally liable for the entity's debts and obligations, such as a corporation, LLC, or LLP.

**limited liability partnership (LLP).** An entity similar to a partnership, but in which the personal liability of each partner is limited. Devised to allow partnerships of lawyers and other professionals limit their personal liability without losing the partnership structure. Does not protect against malpractice or professional responsibility.

**limited partnership.** A legal entity that is somewhat similar to a partnership. In a limited partnership, there are one or more general partner(s), who do not enjoy limited liability status, and one or more limited partners, who do. The limited partners cannot participate in the running of the entity's business or their limited liability status will be jeopardized.

# M

**Massachusetts Commission Against Discrimination (MCAD).** State agency responsible for enforcing the state's anti-discrimination laws.

**Massachusetts Department of Revenue (DOR).** The state agency responsible for collecting state taxes, enforcing state tax laws, and educating the public about state tax requirements.

# N

**noncompete.** A contract restricting the right of a person to compete against another, usually a former employer. Also used by buyers of businesses to keep the business seller from competing.

**nonprofit corporation.** A corporation formed under a separate set of laws than those for business corporations, usually used by churches, condominium associations, and other groups not seeking profits.

# P

**partnership.** An arrangement between two or more persons who agree to pool talent and money and share profits or losses, for the purpose of undertaking some sort of business.

**patent.** A property right granted by the government to an inventor to exclude others from making, using, offering for sale, or selling the invention in a territory or importing the invention into the territory for a limited time in exchange for public disclosure of the invention when the patent is granted.

**piercing the corporate veil.** A legal remedy that can be used to obtain assets of a company's shareholders or equity owners to satisfy a judgment against the company. With it the equity owners of a corporation or limited liability company are held personally liable for the company's debts and liabilities. A court will only allow the *piercing of the veil* in limited circumstances. Some of the factors which may lead a court to *pierce the veil* are commingling of personal and company assets; failure to observe company formalities; failing to hold oneself out to the public as a limited liability entity; undercapitalization; use of company assets for personal purposes; and failure to make legally required filings.

**private placement.** An offer and sale of securities by an entity to a limited number or category of persons.

**professional corporation.** A corporation owned and run by certain professionals such as accountants, lawyers, and doctors. Most states allow certain professionals to incorporate only as a professional corporation. Although the corporation does have limited liability status, it does not protect the professionals from malpractice liability nor does it alter professional responsibility or privilege.

**proprietorship.** A business owned and run by one person, and not incorporated or otherwise enjoying limited liability protection.

# S

**S corporation.** A corporation that has made an official election under federal law to be treated similarly to a partnership for purposes of tax law. The tax attributes of the corporation flow through to its equity owners and are taxed only at the owner level. This is called *flow-through* taxation. In certain states, a state-level filing is also required for the corporation to receive the same tax treatment at the state level.

**service mark.** Same thing as a trademark, except that it identifies and distinguishes the source of a service rather than a product.

**shareholders' agreement.** *See buy-sell agreement.*

# T

**territory.** Area covered by a contract, covenant, license, right, or the like, such as a noncompete or patent.

**trade name.** *See business certificate.*

**trademark.** Any word, name, symbol, or device, or any combination, used, or intended to be used, in commerce to identify and distinguish the goods of one manufacturer or seller from goods manufactured or sold by others, and to indicate the source of the goods. A brand name.

# U

**Uniform Commercial Code (UCC).** A set of laws adopted by almost every state in the U.S. (with variations), governing sales of goods, secured transactions, and other commercial matters.

**usury.** Interest charged at a rate which is excessive or higher than that allowed by law.

# APPENDIX A: SAMPLE FILLED-IN FORMS

The following forms may be photocopied or removed from this book and used immediately. Some of the tax forms explained in this book are not included here because you should use original returns provided by the IRS or the Massachusetts Department of Revenue. Be sure to check with the proper authorities in case there are any additional requirements.

Fee: $50.00

# The Commonwealth of Massachusetts

**William Francis Galvin**
Secretary of the Commonwealth
One Ashburton Place, Boston, Massachusetts 02108-1512

## APPLICATION FOR REGISTRATION OF A TRADEMARK
### (General Laws, Chapter 110B, Section 2)

1. Name of applicant: Mickey the Marble Bengal, Inc.

2. (a) Principal business address: 2 Wildlife Dr., Marlborough, MA 12345

   (b) *Business address in Massachusetts, if any:

3. State whether applicant is an individual, partnership, corporation, union or association: Corporation

4. If a corporation, the state of incorporation is: Massachusetts

5. Describe mark: Mickey's Marbles

6. Describe the specific goods in connection with which the mark is used: Marbles

7. Class No.: 28

8. The mark is used by displaying it:

   ☐ directly to the goods                    ☒ to tags or labels affixed to the containers for the goods
   ☐ directly to the containers for the goods  ☐ to tags or labels affixed directly to the goods
   ☐ by displaying it in physical association with the goods in the sale or distribution thereof
   ☐ in other fashions (explain):

9. Date of first use of mark by applicant or predecessor. If first use of mark was in Massachusetts, use the same date in both (a) and (b).

   (a) Anywhere: 3/11/04

   (b) In Massachusetts: 3/11/04

10. If either of the above first uses was by a predecessor of the applicant, state which use or uses were by a predecessor and identify that predecessor:

State of: _____Massachusetts_____

County of: _____Middlesex_____

Name of applicant: __Mickey the Marble Bengal, Inc.__

Signature of applicant: ___*Mickey Flemming, Pres.*___

Title: _____President_____

**Note: This document must be notarized – see reverse side.**
*Fill in only if principal business address is not in Massachusetts

110bcrtm

_____ , being duly sworn, deposes and says that he is the _____ of the above named applicant, that the statements contained in the foregoing statement are true and that he verily believes that said applicant is the owner of the mark sought to be registered and that no other person has the right in the Commonwealth of Massachusetts to use such mark either in the identical form thereof, or in such near resemblance thereto, as to be likely, when applied to the goods or services of such person, to cause confusion or to cause mistake or to deceive.

SUBSCRIBED and sworn to before me this _____ day of _____ , 20 _____.

Notary Public: _____ My commission expires: _____

*Please print the name and address in the space provided below of the person to whom you wish this application to be sent.

**CERTIFICATE OF REGISTRATION OF A TRADEMARK**

General Laws, Chapter 110B, Section 4

Filed with
William Francis Galvin,
Secretary of the Commonwealth
and Secretary's Certificate of Record issued on:

, 20 _____

William Francis Galvin
Secretary of the Commonwealth
Trademark Section
One Ashburton Place, Rm. 1712
Boston, MA 02108

\* Mickey Flemming _____

2 Wildlife Dr. _____

Marlborough, MA 12345 _____

_____

# INSTRUCTIONS
PLEASE READ ALL INSTRUCTIONS CAREFULLY BEFORE COMPLETING THIS FORM.

**Anti-Discrimination Notice.** It is illegal to discriminate against any individual (other than an alien not authorized to work in the U.S.) in hiring, discharging, or recruiting or referring for a fee because of that individual's national origin or citizenship status. It is illegal to discriminate against work eligible individuals. Employers **CANNOT** specify which document(s) they will accept from an employee. The refusal to hire an individual because of a future expiration date may also constitute illegal discrimination.

## Section 1 - Employee.
All employees, citizens and noncitizens, hired after November 6, 1986, must complete Section 1 of this form at the time of hire, which is the actual beginning of employment. **The employer is responsible for ensuring that Section 1 is timely and properly completed.**

**Preparer/Translator Certification.** The Preparer/Translator Certification must be completed if Section 1 is prepared by a person other than the employee. A preparer/translator may be used only when the employee is unable to complete Section 1 on his/her own. However, the employee must still sign Section 1.

## Section 2 - Employer.
For the purpose of completing this form, the term "employer" includes those recruiters and referrers for a fee who are agricultural associations, agricultural employers or farm labor contractors.

Employers must complete Section 2 by examining evidence of identity and employment eligibility within three (3) business days of the date employment begins. If employees are authorized to work, but are unable to present the required document(s) within three business days, they must present a receipt for the application of the document(s) within three business days and the actual document(s) within ninety (90) days. However, if employers hire individuals for a duration of less than three business days, Section 2 must be completed at the time employment begins. **Employers must record: 1)** document title; **2)** issuing authority; **3)** document number, **4)** expiration date, if any; and **5)** the date employment begins. Employers must sign and date the certification. Employees must present original documents. Employers may, but are not required to, photocopy the document(s) presented. These photocopies may only be used for the verification process and must be retained with the I-9. **However, employers are still responsible for completing the I-9.**

## Section 3 - Updating and Reverification.
Employers must complete Section 3 when updating and/or reverifying the I-9. Employers must reverify employment eligibility of their employees on or before the expiration date recorded in Section 1. Employers **CANNOT** specify which document(s) they will accept from an employee.

- If an employee's name has changed at the time this form is being updated/ reverified, complete Block A.

- If an employee is rehired within three (3) years of the date this form was originally completed and the employee is still eligible to be employed on the same basis as previously indicated on this form (updating), complete Block B and the signature block.

- If an employee is rehired within three (3) years of the date this form was originally completed and the employee's work authorization has expired **or** if a current employee's work authorization is about to expire (reverification), complete Block B and:
  - examine any document that reflects that the employee is authorized to work in the U.S. (see List A **or** C).
  - record the document title, document number and expiration date (if any) in Block C, and complete the signature block.

**Photocopying and Retaining Form I-9.** A blank I-9 may be reproduced, provided both sides are copied. The Instructions must be available to all employees completing this form. Employers must retain completed I-9s for three (3) years after the date of hire or one (1) year after the date employment ends, whichever is later.

**For more detailed information, you may refer to the INS Handbook for Employers, (Form M-274). You may obtain the handbook at your local INS office.**

**Privacy Act Notice.** The authority for collecting this information is the Immigration Reform and Control Act of 1986, Pub. L. 99-603 (8 USC 1324a).

This information is for employers to verify the eligibility of individuals for employment to preclude the unlawful hiring, or recruiting or referring for a fee, of aliens who are not authorized to work in the United States.

This information will be used by employers as a record of their basis for determining eligibility of an employee to work in the United States. The form will be kept by the employer and made available for inspection by officials of the U.S. Immigration and Naturalization Service, the Department of Labor and the Office of Special Counsel for Immigration Related Unfair Employment Practices.

Submission of the information required in this form is voluntary. However, an individual may not begin employment unless this form is completed, since employers are subject to civil or criminal penalties if they do not comply with the Immigration Reform and Control Act of 1986.

**Reporting Burden.** We try to create forms and instructions that are accurate, can be easily understood and which impose the least possible burden on you to provide us with information. Often this is difficult because some immigration laws are very complex. Accordingly, the reporting burden for this collection of information is computed as follows: **1)** learning about this form, 5 minutes; **2)** completing the form, 5 minutes; and **3)** assembling and filing (recordkeeping) the form, 5 minutes, for an average of 15 minutes per response. If you have comments regarding the accuracy of this burden estimate, or suggestions for making this form simpler, you can write to the Immigration and Naturalization Service, HQPDI, 425 I Street, N.W., Room 4034, Washington, DC 20536. OMB No. 1115-0136.

**U.S. Department of Justice**
Immigration and Naturalization Service

OMB No. 1115-0136

# Employment Eligibility Verification

Form I-9 (Rev. 11-21-91)N Page 2

**Please read instructions carefully before completing this form. The instructions must be available during completion of this form. ANTI-DISCRIMINATION NOTICE: It is illegal to discriminate against work eligible individuals. Employers CANNOT specify which document(s) they will accept from an employee. The refusal to hire an individual because of a future expiration date may also constitute illegal discrimination.**

**Section 1. Employee Information and Verification.** To be completed and signed by employee at the time employment begins.

| Print Name: Last | First | Middle Initial | Maiden Name |
|---|---|---|---|
| ANDREWS | DOUGLAS | F. | |

| Address (Street Name and Number) | Apt. # | Date of Birth (month/day/year) |
|---|---|---|
| 12 PORTOBELLO ROAD | | 05/08/64 |

| City | State | Zip Code | Social Security # |
|---|---|---|---|
| EDINBURGH | MA | 55555 | 555-66-2222 |

I am aware that federal law provides for imprisonment and/or fines for false statements or use of false documents in connection with the completion of this form.

I attest, under penalty of perjury, that I am (check one of the following):
- [X] A citizen or national of the United States
- [ ] A Lawful Permanent Resident (Alien # A
- [ ] An alien authorized to work until ___/___/___
(Alien # or Admission #)

| Employee's Signature *Douglas F. Andrews* | Date (month/day/year) 01/29/04 |
|---|---|

**Preparer and/or Translator Certification.** *(To be completed and signed if Section 1 is prepared by a person other than the employee.) I attest, under penalty of perjury, that I have assisted in the completion of this form and that to the best of my knowledge the information is true and correct.*

| Preparer's/Translator's Signature | Print Name |
|---|---|
| | |

| Address (Street Name and Number, City, State, Zip Code) | Date (month/day/year) |
|---|---|
| | |

**Section 2. Employer Review and Verification.** To be completed and signed by employer. Examine one document from List A OR examine one document from List B and one from List C, as listed on the reverse of this form, and record the title, number and expiration date, if any, of the document(s)

| List A | OR | List B | AND | List C |
|---|---|---|---|---|
| Document title: PASSPORT | | | | |
| Issuing authority: PASSPORT AGENCY PTB | | | | |
| Document #: 123456789 | | | | |
| Expiration Date (if any): 10/05/06 | | ___/___/___ | | ___/___/___ |
| Document #: | | | | |
| Expiration Date (if any): ___/___/___ | | | | |

**CERTIFICATION - I attest, under penalty of perjury, that I have examined the document(s) presented by the above-named employee, that the above-listed document(s) appear to be genuine and to relate to the employee named, that the employee began employment on** (month/day/year) 02/03/04 **and that to the best of my knowledge the employee is eligible to work in the United States. (State employment agencies may omit the date the employee began employment.)**

| Signature of Employer or Authorized Representative *Darron Krebbs* | Print Name Darron Krebbs | Title owner |
|---|---|---|

| Business or Organization Name Krebbs Company | Address (Street Name and Number, City, State, Zip Code) 100 Maynard Dr., Edinburgh, MA 55554 | Date (month/day/year) 2/3/04 |
|---|---|---|

**Section 3. Updating and Reverification.** To be completed and signed by employer.

| A. New Name (if applicable) | B. Date of rehire (month/day/year) (if applicable) |
|---|---|
| | |

C. If employee's previous grant of work authorization has expired, provide the information below for the document that establishes current employment eligibility.

Document Title: _____ Document #: _____ Expiration Date (if any): ___/___/___

**I attest, under penalty of perjury, that to the best of my knowledge, this employee is eligible to work in the United States, and if the employee presented document(s), the document(s) I have examined appear to be genuine and to relate to the individual.**

| Signature of Employer or Authorized Representative | Date (month/day/year) |
|---|---|
| | |

# LISTS OF ACCEPTABLE DOCUMENTS

| LIST A | | LIST B | | LIST C |
|---|---|---|---|---|
| **Documents that Establish Both Identity and Employment Eligibility** | **OR** | **Documents that Establish Identity** | **AND** | **Documents that Establish Employment Eligibility** |

### LIST A — Documents that Establish Both Identity and Employment Eligibility

1. U.S. Passport (unexpired or expired)

2. Certificate of U.S. Citizenship (INS Form N-560 or N-561)

3. Certificate of Naturalization (INS Form N-550 or N-570)

4. Unexpired foreign passport, with I-551 stamp or attached INS Form I-94 indicating unexpired employment authorization

5. Permanent Resident Card or Alien Registration Receipt Card with photograph (INS Form I-151 or I-551)

6. Unexpired Temporary Resident Card (INS Form I-688)

7. Unexpired Employment Authorization Card (INS Form I-688A)

8. Unexpired Reentry Permit (INS Form I-327)

9. Unexpired Refugee Travel Document (INS Form I-571)

10. Unexpired Employment Authorization Document issued by the INS which contains a photograph (INS Form I-688B)

### LIST B — Documents that Establish Identity

1. Driver's license or ID card issued by a state or outlying possession of the United States provided it contains a photograph or information such as name, date of birth, gender, height, eye color and address

2. ID card issued by federal, state or local government agencies or entities, provided it contains a photograph or information such as name, date of birth, gender, height, eye color and address

3. School ID card with a photograph

4. Voter's registration card

5. U.S. Military card or draft record

6. Military dependent's ID card

7. U.S. Coast Guard Merchant Mariner Card

8. Native American tribal document

9. Driver's license issued by a Canadian government authority

**For persons under age 18 who are unable to present a document listed above:**

10. School record or report card

11. Clinic, doctor or hospital record

12. Day-care or nursery school record

### LIST C — Documents that Establish Employment Eligibility

1. U.S. social security card issued by the Social Security Administration (other than a card stating it is not valid for employment)

2. Certification of Birth Abroad issued by the Department of State (Form FS-545 or Form DS-1350)

3. Original or certified copy of a birth certificate issued by a state, county, municipal authority or outlying possession of the United States bearing an official seal

4. Native American tribal document

5. U.S. Citizen ID Card (INS Form I-197)

6. ID Card for use of Resident Citizen in the United States (INS Form I-179)

7. Unexpired employment authorization document issued by the INS (other than those listed under List A)

**Illustrations of many of these documents appear in Part 8 of the Handbook for Employers (M-274)**

Form **SS-4**

(Rev. December 2001)

Department of the Treasury
Internal Revenue Service

## Application for Employer Identification Number

(For use by employers, corporations, partnerships, trusts, estates, churches, government agencies, Indian tribal entities, certain individuals, and others.)

▶ See separate instructions for each line.     ▶ Keep a copy for your records.

EIN

OMB No. 1545-0003

*Type or print clearly.*

**1** Legal name of entity (or individual) for whom the EIN is being requested
Ollie the Hound Dog, Inc.

**2** Trade name of business (if different from name on line 1)
n/a

**3** Executor, trustee, "care of" name

**4a** Mailing address (room, apt., suite no. and street, or P.O. box)
1 Always Underfoot Road

**4b** City, state, and ZIP code
Holliston, MA 01746

**5a** Street address (if different) (Do not enter a P.O. box.)

**5b** City, state, and ZIP code

**6** County and state where principal business is located
Middlesex, MA

**7a** Name of principal officer, general partner, grantor, owner, or trustor
Ollie D. Goofball

**7b** SSN, ITIN, or EIN     999-99-9999

**8a** **Type of entity** (check only one box)
- [X] Sole proprietor (SSN) _____
- [ ] Partnership
- [ ] Corporation (enter form number to be filed) ▶ _____
- [ ] Personal service corp.
- [ ] Church or church-controlled organization
- [ ] Other nonprofit organization (specify) ▶ _____
- [ ] Other (specify) ▶

- [ ] Estate (SSN of decedent) _____
- [ ] Plan administrator (SSN) _____
- [ ] Trust (SSN of grantor) _____
- [ ] National Guard     [ ] State/local government
- [ ] Farmers' cooperative     [ ] Federal government/military
- [ ] REMIC     [ ] Indian tribal governments/enterprises
- Group Exemption Number (GEN) ▶ _____

**8b** If a corporation, name the state or foreign country (if applicable) where incorporated

State

Foreign country

**9** **Reason for applying** (check only one box)
- [X] Started new business (specify type) ▶ _____
  bark sales
- [ ] Hired employees (Check the box and see line 12.)
- [ ] Compliance with IRS withholding regulations
- [ ] Other (specify) ▶

- [ ] Banking purpose (specify purpose) ▶ _____
- [ ] Changed type of organization (specify new type) ▶ _____
- [ ] Purchased going business
- [ ] Created a trust (specify type) ▶ _____
- [ ] Created a pension plan (specify type) ▶ _____

**10** Date business started or acquired (month, day, year)
10-15-2004

**11** Closing month of accounting year
December

**12** First date wages or annuities were paid or will be paid (month, day, year). **Note:** If applicant is a withholding agent, enter date income will first be paid to nonresident alien. (month, day, year) . . . . . . . . . . . . . . ▶

**13** Highest number of employees expected in the next 12 months. **Note:** If the applicant does not expect to have any employees during the period, enter "-0-." . . . . . . . . . . . ▶

| Agricultural | Household | Other |
|---|---|---|
|  |  |  |

**14** Check **one** box that best describes the principal activity of your business.
- [ ] Construction     [ ] Rental & leasing     [ ] Transportation & warehousing
- [ ] Real estate     [ ] Manufacturing     [ ] Finance & insurance

- [ ] Health care & social assistance     [X] Wholesale–agent/broker
- [ ] Accommodation & food service     [ ] Wholesale–other     [ ] Retail
- [ ] Other (specify)

**15** Indicate principal line of merchandise sold; specific construction work done; products produced; or services provided.
bark sales

**16a** Has the applicant ever applied for an employer identification number for this or any other business? . . . . . [X] Yes     [ ] No
**Note:** If "Yes," please complete lines 16b and 16c.

**16b** If you checked "Yes" on line 16a, give applicant's legal name and trade name shown on prior application if different from line 1 or 2 above.
Legal name ▶               Trade name ▶

**16c** Approximate date when, and city and state where, the application was filed. Enter previous employer identification number if known.

| Approximate date when filed (mo., day, year) | City and state where filed | Previous EIN |
|---|---|---|
|  |  |  |

Complete this section **only** if you want to authorize the named individual to receive the entity's EIN and answer questions about the completion of this form.

**Third Party Designee**

Designee's name
Ollie D. Goofball, owner

Designee's telephone number (include area code)
( 518 ) 555-0000

Address and ZIP code

Designee's fax number (include area code)
(     )

Under penalties of perjury, I declare that I have examined this application, and to the best of my knowledge and belief, it is true, correct, and complete.

Applicant's telephone number (include area code)
(     )

Name and title (type or print clearly) ▶

Signature ▶ *Ollie D. Goofball*     Date ▶ 10/20/2004

Applicant's fax number (include area code)
(     )

For Privacy Act and Paperwork Reduction Act Notice, see separate instructions.     Cat. No. 16055N     Form **SS-4** (Rev. 12-2001)

| M-942 | MASSACHUSETTS DEPARTMENT OF REVENUE | | | | |
|---|---|---|---|---|---|

**W42** EMPLOYER'S MONTHLY RETURN OF INCOME TAXES WITHHELD
YOU MUST FILE THIS FORM EVEN THOUGH NO TAX MAY BE DUE.

| | | | NUMBER OF EMPLOYEES FROM WHOM TAXES WERE WITHHELD: | 3 |
|---|---|---|---|---|

FEDERAL IDENTIFICATION NUMBER | BE SURE THIS RETURN COVERS THE CORRECT PERIOD | FOR MONTH/YEAR
04-5555555

| | | |
|---|---|---|
| **1. AMOUNT WITHHELD** | 250.00 | |

IF ANY INFOR-MATION IS INCORRECT, SEE INSTRUC-TIONS.

Everett & Luke's Catnip, Inc.
7 Huckleberry Lane
Oliver, MA 99999

| | | |
|---|---|---|
| **2. ADJUSTMENT FOR PRIOR AMOUNT WITHHELD\*** | | |

☐ Check here if this is a final return.  ☐ Check here if EFT payment.

| | | |
|---|---|---|
| **3. AMOUNT DUE AFTER ADJUST-MENT (NOT LESS THAN "0")** | | |
| **4. PENALTIES** | | |
| **5. INTEREST** | | |
| **6. TOTAL AMOUNT DUE (ADD LINES 3, 4 AND 5)** | 250.00 | |

Return is due with payment on or before the 15th day of the month following the month indicated above, except during March, June, September and December — then due the last day of the following month. Make check payable to Commonwealth of Massachusetts. Mail to: **Massachusetts Department of Revenue, PO Box 7038, Boston, MA 02204.**

CHECK HERE IF USING THE BACK OF THIS FORM: ☐

I declare under the penalties of perjury that this return (including any accompanying schedules and statements) has been examined by me and to the best of my knowledge and belief is a true, correct and complete return.

\*Explain any adjustment on reverse or it will be disallowed.

Signature *Everett O'Neill*    Title *President*    Date *6/5/05*

---

**New owners — do not use previous owner's form to file your return. Any change in ownership or organization requires a new registration. You must file a new Form TA-1.**

| LINE 2 ADJUSTMENT INFORMATION | | | STATE REASON FOR ADJUSTMENT REQUEST: |
|---|---|---|---|
| | AS REPORTED | CORRECTED | |
| AMOUNT WITHHELD | | | |
| ADJUSTMENT PRIOR PERIOD | | | |
| AMOUNT PAID | | | |
| REPORTED UNDER FED. IDENT. NO. | | | |
| REPORTING PERIOD IN ERROR | | | |

88M 7/00 00-B02

♻ *printed on recycled paper*

**MASSACHUSETTS DIVISION OF UNEMPLOYMENT ASSISTANCE**

## EMPLOYER STATUS REPORT

Complete And Return This Form Within 10 days To:
Status Department - 5th Floor
19 Staniford Street
Boston, MA 02114-2589

**PLEASE TYPE OR PRINT CLEARLY IN INK.**

**ALSO COMPLETE REVERSE SIDE.**
**CALL (617) 626-5075 FOR ASSISTANCE.**

Name of employing unit: **Dug's Rugs, Inc.**       Trade name: **none**

List **ALL** business locations in Massachusetts. If more than one attach a separate sheet.

**13 Oriental Lane**                **Sherborn**      **MA**      **99776**
No.   Street (do not use P.O. box number)      City              State      Zip Code

Mailing address:                           Address where you keep your payroll records:
No.   St./P.O. box no.   City   State   Zip Code      **same**

Business phone: **508**   **555-6678**        Federal identification no.: **04-3333333**
Area Code       Number

Owner, partners or officers:

| Name | S.S.A. No. | Home address (do not use P.O. box numbers) | Title | Are officers compensated for their services? |
|---|---|---|---|---|
| Dug Andrews | 444-55-6666 | 3 Edinburgh St. Portobello, MA 88993 | Pres. | X Yes ☐ No |
| | | | | ☐ Yes ☐ No |
| | | | | ☐ Yes ☐ No |

Type of organization: ☐ Individual  ☐ Partnership  ☐ Corporation  **X** Other (specify) _____
If corporation:   date incorporated **1/6/05**   state **MA**

First date of employment in Massachusetts: **1/13/05**

Are you a client of an employee leasing company? ☐ Yes  **X** No
If yes, name of employee leasing company _____

Are you liable for federal unemployment tax?
☐ Yes  **X** No   1st date of liability _____

Have you previously been subject to the Massachusetts Employment and Training Law?  ☐ Yes  **X** No
If yes, give account number _____ name _____

Do you hold an exemption from federal income taxes as a non-profit organization described under section 501 (c)(3) of the Internal Revenue Code?  ☐ Yes  **X** No
If Yes, please attach a copy of your exemption with this report.

Describe nature of your company's business/industry:
**Oriental rug sales**

Specify your principal activity. Name your principal commodity, product or service.
**Oriental rug sales**

If your main activity in Massachusetts is to provide support services to other locations of your company, please check appropriate box:
☐ Headquarters    ☐ Research    ☐ Warehouse
☐ Computer Center    ☐ Other (specify) _____

Did you acquire the business of a predecessor?   ☐ Yes  **X** No   If Yes, state:   date acquired: _____
Name of predecessor: _____   Predecessor DUA account number: _____
Did you acquire **ALL** or **PART** of the business of the predecessor?   ☐ ALL   ☐ PART
Acquisition of one of several locations in Massachusetts is considered **PART** of the business.
How acquired?   ☐ Purchase   ☐ Lease   ☐ Franchise   ☐ Other   (explain) _____
Did you acquire the assets of the predecessor's business?   ☐ Yes   ☐ No
Describe those assets acquired:

Describe those assets **NOT** acquired:

Will the predecessor remain in business in Massachusetts?   ☐ Yes   ☐ No   If No, give the date of last payroll: _____
If **Yes**, what is present Massachusetts location of predecessor? _____

Number of Employees: _____
No.   Street   City   State   Zip Code

**DOMESTIC EMPLOYERS:**
Did you pay $1,000 or more in cash remuneration in any calendar quarter during the current or preceding calendar year for domestic services?   ☐ Yes   ☐ No

**AGRICULTURAL EMPLOYERS:**
Did you pay $20,000 or more in cash remuneration for agricultural services during any calendar quarter of the current or preceding calendar year?   ☐ Yes   ☐ No

Did you employ 10 or more individuals on some day in each of 20 calendar weeks, not necessarily consecutive, in either the current or preceding calendar year?   ☐ Yes   ☐ No

**ALL OTHER EMPLOYERS:**
Did you pay wages of $1,500 or more in any calendar quarter in either the current or preceding calendar year?   ☒ Yes   ☐ No

Did you employ one or more individuals on some day in each of 13 weeks, not necessarily consecutive, in either the current or preceding calendar year?   ☒ Yes   ☐ No

If an "OUT OF STATE" employer, did you have a Massachusetts payroll in excess of $200?   ☐ Yes   ☐ No

List below the number of individuals in your employ in Massachusetts within each calendar week. Include full and part time employees, also paid officers if a corporation. An individual proprietor or a partner should not be counted as an employee. Show total Massachusetts payroll for each calendar quarter.

2004

| RECORD OF MASSACHUSETTS EMPLOYMENT IN CURRENT CALENDAR YEAR | | | | | | | | | | | | | | | ENTER YEAR | | | |
|---|---|---|---|---|---|---|---|---|---|---|---|---|---|---|---|---|---|---|
| | JANUARY | | | FEBRUARY | | | | MARCH | | | | APRIL | | | MAY | | | JUNE | |
| Week Ending | 17 | 24 | 31 | 7 | 14 | 21 | 28 | 7 | 14 | 21 | 28 | | | | | | | | |
| Number Employed | 2 | 2 | 2 | 2 | 2 | 2 | | 2 | 2 | 2 | | | | | | | | | |
| | JULY | | | AUGUST | | | | SEPTEMBER | | | | OCTOBER | | | NOVEMBER | | | DECEMBER | |
| Week Ending | | | | | | | | | | | | | | | | | | | |
| Number Employed | | | | | | | | | | | | | | | | | | | |

TOTAL WAGES     1st QTR. $          2nd QTR. $          3rd QTR. $          4th QTR. $

| RECORD OF MASSACHUSETTS EMPLOYMENT IN PRECEDING CALENDAR YEAR | | | | | | | | | | | | | | | ENTER YEAR _____ | | | |
|---|---|---|---|---|---|---|---|---|---|---|---|---|---|---|---|---|---|---|
| | JANUARY | | | FEBRUARY | | | | MARCH | | | | APRIL | | | MAY | | | JUNE | |
| Week Ending | | | | | | | | | | | | | | | | | | | |
| Number Employed | | | | | | | | | | | | | | | | | | | |
| | JULY | | | AUGUST | | | | SEPTEMBER | | | | OCTOBER | | | NOVEMBER | | | DECEMBER | |
| Week Ending | | | | | | | | | | | | | | | | | | | |
| Number Employed | | | | | | | | | | | | | | | | | | | |

TOTAL WAGES     1st QTR. $          2nd QTR. $          3rd QTR. $          4th QTR. $

| RECORD OF MASSACHUSETTS EMPLOYMENT IN PRECEDING CALENDAR YEAR | | | | | | | | | | | | | | | ENTER YEAR _____ | | | |
|---|---|---|---|---|---|---|---|---|---|---|---|---|---|---|---|---|---|---|
| | JANUARY | | | FEBRUARY | | | | MARCH | | | | APRIL | | | MAY | | | JUNE | |
| Week Ending | | | | | | | | | | | | | | | | | | | |
| Number Employed | | | | | | | | | | | | | | | | | | | |
| | JULY | | | AUGUST | | | | SEPTEMBER | | | | OCTOBER | | | NOVEMBER | | | DECEMBER | |
| Week Ending | | | | | | | | | | | | | | | | | | | |
| Number Employed | | | | | | | | | | | | | | | | | | | |

TOTAL WAGES     1st QTR. $          2nd QTR. $          3rd QTR. $          4th QTR. $

**PREDECESSOR: I hereby certify that all information submitted by the successor is true in accordance with the transfer.**

Signature: _____     Title: _____
owner, partner or officer

**THIS REPORT MUST BE SIGNED BY THE OWNER, A PARTNER OR CORPORATE OFFICER**
I certify, under penalties of perjury, that all statements made hereon are true to the best of my knowledge and belief.

Name of employing unit: Dug's Rugs, Inc.          Date: 3/31/05

Signature: *Dug Andrews*          Title: President

1110-A Rev. 02-04

# APPENDIX B:
# TAX TIMETABLE AND
# READY-TO-USE FORMS

The following forms may be photocopied or removed from this book and used immediately. Some of the tax forms explained in this book are not included here because you should use original returns provided by the IRS (940, 941) or the Massachusetts Department of Revenue (quarterly unemployment compensation form). Be sure to check with the proper authorities in case there are any additional requirements.

# FEDERAL TAX TIMETABLE

| | ESTIMATED PAYMENT | ANNUAL RETURN | FORM 941* | MISC. |
|---|---|---|---|---|
| JAN. | 15th | | 31st | 31st<br>940    W-2<br>508    1099 |
| FEB. | | | | 28th<br>W-3 |
| MAR | | 15th<br>Corp. &<br>Partnership | | 30th<br>508 |
| APR. | 15th | | 30th | |
| MAY | | | | |
| JUN. | 15th | 15th<br>Personal | | |
| JUL. | | | 31st | 31st<br>508 |
| AUG. | | | | |
| SEP. | 15th | | | |
| OCT. | | | 31st | 31st<br>508 |
| NOV. | | | | |
| DEC. | | | | |

* In addition to form 941, deposits must be made regularly if withholding exceeds $500 in any month.

# CITY OF _____
# MASSACHUSETTS

### Certificate Stating Real Name of Person Transacting Business

Date: _____

**To the City Clerk:**

In conformity with the provisions of MGL chapter 110, Section 5, Notice is hereby given that business is being conducted under the name of:

Business name:

_____

Proposed Use (please describe): _____

Location of Business: _____

The nearest cross street: _____and_____

The full name and address of each person conducting such business:

Name: _____ Address: _____

Name: _____ Address: _____

Name: _____ Address: _____

Signed: _____

_____

_____

_____

_____, SS          Date: _____

Then personally appeared the above named: _____

(affix seal here)

_____

and made oath that the foregoing are true before me,

Signed: _____

Title: _____

Please indicate here if the business in a "home business": **YES/NO** (circle one)

**PLEASE NOTE:** If the proposed business is to be located in a residence you must first go to the Inspectional Services Department and fill out a "Home Business Affidavit" thereby acknowledging compliance with the Home Business Ordinance.

I hereby certify that the above business address is in the following zoning district, and is an allowed use in accordance with the Revised Zoning Ordinances of the City of _____.

Zoning District: _____     Attest: _____
                                                                Inspectional Services Dept.
                                                                    Official

Received: Date: _____     Time: _____

and entered in Records of Business Titles in the City Clerk's Office in the City of _____.

               Book: _____     Page: _____

                                            _____

                                    _____ City Clerk

Fee: $50.00

# The Commonwealth of Massachusetts
**William Francis Galvin**
Secretary of the Commonwealth
One Ashburton Place, Boston, Massachusetts 02108-1512

## APPLICATION FOR REGISTRATION OF A TRADEMARK
(General Laws, Chapter 110B, Section 2)

1. Name of applicant:

2. (a) Principal business address:

   (b) *Business address in Massachusetts, if any:

3. State whether applicant is an individual, partnership, corporation, union or association:

4. If a corporation, the state of incorporation is:

5. Describe mark:

6. Describe the specific goods in connection with which the mark is used:

7. Class No.:

8. The mark is used by displaying it:

   ☐ directly to the goods             ☐ to tags or labels affixed to the containers for the goods
   ☐ directly to the containers for the goods     ☐ to tags or labels affixed directly to the goods
   ☐ by displaying it in physical association with the goods in the sale or distribution thereof
   ☐ in other fashions (explain):

9. Date of first use of mark by applicant or predecessor. If first use of mark was in Massachusetts, use the same date in both (a) and (b).

   (a) Anywhere:

   (b) In Massachusetts:

10. If either of the above first uses was by a predecessor of the applicant, state which use or uses were by a predecessor and identify that predecessor:

Name of applicant: _____

State of: _____

Signature of applicant: _____

County of: _____

Title: _____

*Note: This document must be notarized — see reverse side.*
*Fill in only if principal business address is not in Massachusetts.*

**U.S. Department of Justice**
Immigration and Naturalization Service

OMB No. 1115-0136

# Employment Eligibility Verification

Please read instructions carefully before completing this form. The instructions must be available during completion of this form. ANTI-DISCRIMINATION NOTICE: It is illegal to discriminate against work eligible individuals. Employers CANNOT specify which document(s) they will accept from an employee. The refusal to hire an individual because of a future expiration date may also constitute illegal discrimination.

**Section 1. Employee Information and Verification.** To be completed and signed by employee at the time employment begins.

| Print Name: Last | First | Middle Initial | Maiden Name |
|---|---|---|---|

| Address (Street Name and Number) | Apt. # | Date of Birth (month/day/year) |
|---|---|---|

| City | State | Zip Code | Social Security # |
|---|---|---|---|

I am aware that federal law provides for imprisonment and/or fines for false statements or use of false documents in connection with the completion of this form.

I attest, under penalty of perjury, that I am (check one of the following):
- [ ] A citizen or national of the United States
- [ ] A Lawful Permanent Resident (Alien # A
- [ ] An alien authorized to work until ___ / ___ / ___
(Alien # or Admission #)

| Employee's Signature | Date (month/day/year) |
|---|---|

**Preparer and/or Translator Certification.** *(To be completed and signed if Section 1 is prepared by a person other than the employee.) I attest, under penalty of perjury, that I have assisted in the completion of this form and that to the best of my knowledge the information is true and correct.*

| Preparer's/Translator's Signature | Print Name |
|---|---|

| Address (Street Name and Number, City, State, Zip Code) | Date (month/day/year) |
|---|---|

**Section 2. Employer Review and Verification.** To be completed and signed by employer. Examine one document from List A OR examine one document from List B and one from List C, as listed on the reverse of this form, and record the title, number and expiration date, if any, of the document(s)

| List A | OR | List B | AND | List C |
|---|---|---|---|---|
| Document title: _____ | | _____ | | _____ |
| Issuing authority: _____ | | _____ | | _____ |
| Document #: _____ | | _____ | | _____ |
| Expiration Date (if any): ___/___/___ | | ___/___/___ | | ___/___/___ |
| Document #: _____ | | | | |
| Expiration Date (if any): ___/___/___ | | | | |

CERTIFICATION - I attest, under penalty of perjury, that I have examined the document(s) presented by the above-named employee, that the above-listed document(s) appear to be genuine and to relate to the employee named, that the employee began employment on (month/day/year) ___/___/___ and that to the best of my knowledge the employee is eligible to work in the United States. (State employment agencies may omit the date the employee began employment.)

| Signature of Employer or Authorized Representative | Print Name | Title |
|---|---|---|

| Business or Organization Name | Address (Street Name and Number, City, State, Zip Code) | Date (month/day/year) |
|---|---|---|

**Section 3. Updating and Reverification.** To be completed and signed by employer.

| A. New Name (if applicable) | B. Date of rehire (month/day/year) (if applicable) |
|---|---|

C. If employee's previous grant of work authorization has expired, provide the information below for the document that establishes current employment eligibility.

Document Title: _____ Document #: _____ Expiration Date (if any): ___/___/___

I attest, under penalty of perjury, that to the best of my knowledge, this employee is eligible to work in the United States, and if the employee presented document(s), the document(s) I have examined appear to be genuine and to relate to the individual.

| Signature of Employer or Authorized Representative | Date (month/day/year) |
|---|---|

# LISTS OF ACCEPTABLE DOCUMENTS

| LIST A | | LIST B | | LIST C |
|---|---|---|---|---|
| **Documents that Establish Both Identity and Employment Eligibility** | **OR** | **Documents that Establish Identity** | **AND** | **Documents that Establish Employment Eligibility** |

**LIST A — Documents that Establish Both Identity and Employment Eligibility**

1. U.S. Passport (unexpired or expired)

2. Certificate of U.S. Citizenship *(INS Form N-560 or N-561)*

3. Certificate of Naturalization *(INS Form N-550 or N-570)*

4. Unexpired foreign passport, with *I-551 stamp or* attached *INS Form I-94* indicating unexpired employment authorization

5. Permanent Resident Card or Alien Registration Receipt Card with photograph *(INS Form I-151 or I-551)*

6. Unexpired Temporary Resident Card *(INS Form I-688)*

7. Unexpired Employment Authorization Card *(INS Form I-688A)*

8. Unexpired Reentry Permit *(INS Form I-327)*

9. Unexpired Refugee Travel Document *(INS Form I-571)*

10. Unexpired Employment Authorization Document issued by the INS which contains a photograph *(INS Form I-688B)*

**LIST B — Documents that Establish Identity**

1. Driver's license or ID card issued by a state or outlying possession of the United States provided it contains a photograph or information such as name, date of birth, gender, height, eye color and address

2. ID card issued by federal, state or local government agencies or entities, provided it contains a photograph or information such as name, date of birth, gender, height, eye color and address

3. School ID card with a photograph

4. Voter's registration card

5. U.S. Military card or draft record

6. Military dependent's ID card

7. U.S. Coast Guard Merchant Mariner Card

8. Native American tribal document

9. Driver's license issued by a Canadian government authority

**For persons under age 18 who are unable to present a document listed above:**

10. School record or report card

11. Clinic, doctor or hospital record

12. Day-care or nursery school record

**LIST C — Documents that Establish Employment Eligibility**

1. U.S. social security card issued by the Social Security Administration *(other than a card stating it is not valid for employment)*

2. Certification of Birth Abroad issued by the Department of State *(Form FS-545 or Form DS-1350)*

3. Original or certified copy of a birth certificate issued by a state, county, municipal authority or outlying possession of the United States bearing an official **seal**

4. Native American tribal document

5. U.S. Citizen ID Card *(INS Form I-197)*

6. ID Card for use of Resident Citizen in the United States *(INS Form I-179)*

7. Unexpired employment authorization document issued by the INS *(other than those listed under List A)*

**Illustrations of many of these documents appear in Part 8 of the Handbook for Employers (M-274)**

*This page intentionally blank*

Form **SS-4**

(Rev. December 2001)

Department of the Treasury
Internal Revenue Service

# Application for Employer Identification Number

(For use by employers, corporations, partnerships, trusts, estates, churches, government agencies, Indian tribal entities, certain individuals, and others.)

▶ See separate instructions for each line.  ▶ Keep a copy for your records.

EIN

OMB No. 1545-0003

Type or print clearly.

**1** Legal name of entity (or individual) for whom the EIN is being requested

**2** Trade name of business (if different from name on line 1)

**3** Executor, trustee, "care of" name

**4a** Mailing address (room, apt., suite no. and street, or P.O. box)

**5a** Street address (if different) (Do not enter a P.O. box.)

**4b** City, state, and ZIP code

**5b** City, state, and ZIP code

**6** County and state where principal business is located

**7a** Name of principal officer, general partner, grantor, owner, or trustor

**7b** SSN, ITIN, or EIN

**8a** **Type of entity** (check only one box)

☐ Sole proprietor (SSN) _____

☐ Partnership

☐ Corporation (enter form number to be filed) ▶ _____

☐ Personal service corp.

☐ Church or church-controlled organization

☐ Other nonprofit organization (specify) ▶ _____

☐ Other (specify) ▶

☐ Estate (SSN of decedent) _____

☐ Plan administrator (SSN) _____

☐ Trust (SSN of grantor) _____

☐ National Guard   ☐ State/local government

☐ Farmers' cooperative   ☐ Federal government/military

☐ REMIC   ☐ Indian tribal governments/enterprises

Group Exemption Number (GEN) ▶ _____

**8b** If a corporation, name the state or foreign country (if applicable) where incorporated

State

Foreign country

**9** **Reason for applying** (check only one box)

☐ Started new business (specify type) ▶ _____

_____

☐ Hired employees (Check the box and see line 12.)

☐ Compliance with IRS withholding regulations

☐ Other (specify) ▶

☐ Banking purpose (specify purpose) ▶ _____

☐ Changed type of organization (specify new type) ▶ _____

☐ Purchased going business

☐ Created a trust (specify type) ▶ _____

☐ Created a pension plan (specify type) ▶ _____

**10** Date business started or acquired (month, day, year)

**11** Closing month of accounting year

**12** First date wages or annuities were paid or will be paid (month, day, year). **Note:** *If applicant is a withholding agent, enter date income will first be paid to nonresident alien. (month, day, year)* . . . . . . . . . . . . . ▶

**13** Highest number of employees expected in the next 12 months. **Note:** *If the applicant does not expect to have any employees during the period, enter "-0-."* . . . . . . . . . . ▶

| Agricultural | Household | Other |
|---|---|---|
| | | |

**14** Check **one** box that best describes the principal activity of your business.

☐ Construction   ☐ Rental & leasing   ☐ Transportation & warehousing   ☐ Health care & social assistance   ☐ Wholesale–agent/broker

☐ Real estate   ☐ Manufacturing   ☐ Finance & insurance   ☐ Accommodation & food service   ☐ Wholesale–other   ☐ Retail

☐ Other (specify)

**15** Indicate principal line of merchandise sold; specific construction work done; products produced; or services provided.

**16a** Has the applicant ever applied for an employer identification number for this or any other business? . . . . . ☐ **Yes**   ☐ **No**

**Note:** *If "Yes," please complete lines 16b and 16c.*

**16b** If you checked "Yes" on line 16a, give applicant's legal name and trade name shown on prior application if different from line 1 or 2 above.

Legal name ▶   Trade name ▶

**16c** Approximate date when, and city and state where, the application was filed. Enter previous employer identification number if known.

Approximate date when filed (mo., day, year)   City and state where filed   Previous EIN

**Third Party Designee**

Complete this section **only** if you want to authorize the named individual to receive the entity's EIN and answer questions about the completion of this form.

Designee's name

Designee's telephone number (include area code)

( )

Address and ZIP code

Designee's fax number (include area code)

( )

Under penalties of perjury, I declare that I have examined this application, and to the best of my knowledge and belief, it is true, correct, and complete.

Applicant's telephone number (include area code)

( )

Name and title (type or print clearly) ▶

Applicant's fax number (include area code)

( )

Signature ▶   Date ▶

For Privacy Act and Paperwork Reduction Act Notice, see separate instructions.   Cat. No. 16055N   Form **SS-4** (Rev. 12-2001)

## Where To Fax or File

| If your principal business, office or agency, or legal residence in the case of an individual, is located in: | Call the Fax-TIN number shown or file with the "Internal Revenue Service Center" at: |
| --- | --- |
| Connecticut, Delaware, District of Columbia, Florida, Georgia, Maine, Maryland, Massachusetts, New Hampshire, New Jersey, New York, North Carolina, Ohio, Pennsylvania, Rhode Island, South Carolina, Vermont, Virginia, West Virginia | Attn: EIN Operation P. O. Box 9003 Holtsville, NY 11742-9003 Fax-TIN 631-447-8960 |
| Illinois, Indiana, Kentucky, Michigan | Attn: EIN Operation Cincinnati, OH 45999 Fax-TIN 859-669-5760 |
| Alabama, Alaska, Arizona, Arkansas, California, Colorado, Hawaii, Idaho, Iowa, Kansas, Louisiana, Minnesota, Mississippi, Missouri, Montana, Nebraska, Nevada, New Mexico, North Dakota, Oklahoma, Oregon, Puerto Rico, South Dakota, Tennessee, Texas, Utah, Washington, Wisconsin, Wyoming | Attn: EIN Operation Philadelphia, PA 19255 Fax-TIN 215-516-3990 |
| If you have no legal residence, principal place of business, or principal office or agency in any state: | Attn: EIN Operation Philadelphia, PA 19255 Telephone 215-516-6999 Fax-TIN 215-516-3990 |

## How To Get Forms and Publications

**Phone.** You can order forms, instructions, and publications by phone 24 hours a day, 7 days a week. Call 1-800-TAX-FORM (1-800-829-3676). You should receive your order or notification of its status within 10 workdays.

**Personal computer.** With your personal computer and modem, you can get the forms and information you need using the IRS website at **www.irs.gov** or File Transfer Protocol at **ftp.irs.gov.**

**CD-ROM.** For small businesses, return preparers, or others who may frequently need tax forms or publications, a CD-ROM containing over 2,000 tax products (including many prior year forms) can be purchased from the National Technical Information Service (NTIS).

To order **Pub. 1796,** Federal Tax Products on CD-ROM, call **1-877-CDFORMS** (1-877-233-6767) toll free or connect to **www.irs.gov/cdorders.**

## Tax Help for Your Business

IRS-sponsored Small Business Workshops provide information about your Federal and state tax obligations. For information about workshops in your area, call 1-800-829-4933.

## Related Forms and Publications

The following **forms** and **instructions** may be useful to filers of Form SS-4:
- **Form 990-T,** Exempt Organization Business Income Tax Return
- **Instructions for Form 990-T**
- **Schedule C (Form 1040),** Profit or Loss From Business
- **Schedule F (Form 1040),** Profit or Loss From Farming
- **Instructions for Form 1041 and Schedules A, B, D, G, I, J, and K-1,** U.S. Income Tax Return for Estates and Trusts
- **Form 1042,** Annual Withholding Tax Return for U.S. Source Income of Foreign Persons
- **Instructions for Form 1065,** U.S. Return of Partnership Income
- **Instructions for Form 1066,** U.S. Real Estate Mortgage Investment Conduit (REMIC) Income Tax Return
- **Instructions for Forms 1120 and 1120-A**
- **Form 2553,** Election by a Small Business Corporation
- **Form 2848,** Power of Attorney and Declaration of Representative
- **Form 8821,** Tax Information Authorization
- **Form 8832,** Entity Classification Election

For more **information** about filing Form SS-4 and related issues, see:
- **Circular A,** Agricultural Employer's Tax Guide (Pub. 51)
- **Circular E,** Employer's Tax Guide (Pub. 15)
- **Pub. 538,** Accounting Periods and Methods
- **Pub. 542,** Corporations
- **Pub. 557,** Exempt Status for Your Organization
- **Pub. 583,** Starting a Business and Keeping Records
- **Pub. 966,** Electronic Choices for Paying ALL Your Federal Taxes
- **Pub. 1635,** Understanding Your EIN
- **Package 1023,** Application for Recognition of Exemption Under Section 501(c)(3) of the Internal Revenue Code
- **Package 1024,** Application for Recognition of Exemption Under Section 501(a)

## Specific Instructions

Print or type all entries on Form SS-4. Follow the instructions for each line to expedite processing and to avoid unnecessary IRS requests for additional information. Enter "N/A" (nonapplicable) on the lines that do not apply.

**Line 1—Legal name of entity (or individual) for whom the EIN is being requested.** Enter the legal name of the entity (or individual) applying for the EIN exactly as it appears on the social security card, charter, or other applicable legal document.

*Individuals.* Enter your first name, middle initial, and last name. If you are a sole proprietor, enter your individual name, not your business name. Enter your business name on line 2. Do not use abbreviations or nicknames on line 1.

**Trusts.** Enter the name of the trust.

**Estate of a decedent.** Enter the name of the estate.

**Partnerships.** Enter the legal name of the partnership as it appears in the partnership agreement.

**Corporations.** Enter the corporate name as it appears in the corporation charter or other legal document creating it.

**Plan administrators.** Enter the name of the plan administrator. A plan administrator who already has an EIN should use that number.

**Line 2—Trade name of business.** Enter the trade name of the business if different from the legal name. The trade name is the "doing business as " (DBA) name.

 *Use the full legal name shown on line 1 on all tax returns filed for the entity. (However, if you enter a trade name on line 2 and choose to use the trade name instead of the legal name, enter the trade name on **all returns** you file.) To prevent processing delays and errors, **always** use the legal name only (or the trade name only) on **all** tax returns.*

**Line 3—Executor, trustee, "care of" name.** Trusts enter the name of the trustee. Estates enter the name of the executor, administrator, or other fiduciary. If the entity applying has a designated person to receive tax information, enter that person's name as the "care of" person. Enter the individual's first name, middle initial, and last name.

**Lines 4a-b—Mailing address.** Enter the mailing address for the entity's correspondence. If line 3 is completed, enter the address for the executor, trustee or "care of" person. Generally, this address will be used on all tax returns.

 *File **Form 8822**, Change of Address, to report any subsequent changes to the entity's mailing address.*

**Lines 5a-b—Street address.** Provide the entity's physical address **only** if different from its mailing address shown in lines 4a-b. **Do not** enter a P.O. box number here.

**Line 6—County and state where principal business is located.** Enter the entity's primary **physical** location.

**Lines 7a-b—Name of principal officer, general partner, grantor, owner, or trustor.** Enter the first name, middle initial, last name, and SSN of **(a)** the principal officer if the business is a corporation, **(b)** a general partner if a partnership, **(c)** the owner of an entity that is disregarded as separate from its owner (disregarded entities owned by a corporation enter the corporation's name and EIN), or **(d)** a grantor, owner, or trustor if a trust.

If the person in question is an **alien individual** with a previously assigned individual taxpayer identification number (ITIN), enter the ITIN in the space provided and submit a copy of an official identifying document. If

necessary, complete **Form W-7,** Application for IRS Individual Taxpayer Identification Number, to obtain an ITIN.

You are **required** to enter an SSN, ITIN, or EIN unless the only reason you are applying for an EIN is to make an entity classification election (see Regulations sections 301.7701-1 through 301.7701-3) and you are a nonresident alien with no effectively connected income from sources within the United States.

**Line 8a—Type of entity.** Check the box that best describes the type of entity applying for the EIN. If you are an alien individual with an ITIN previously assigned to you, enter the ITIN in place of a requested SSN.

 *This is not an election for a tax classification of an entity. See **Limited liability company (LLC)** on page 4.*

**Other.** If not specifically listed, check the "Other" box, enter the type of entity and the type of return, if any, that will be filed (for example, "Common Trust Fund, Form 1065" or "Created a Pension Plan"). Do not enter "N/A." If you are an alien individual applying for an EIN, see the **Lines 7a-b** instructions above.

● **Household employer.** If you are an individual, check the "Other" box and enter "Household Employer" and your SSN. If you are a state or local agency serving as a tax reporting agent for public assistance recipients who become household employers, check the "Other" box and enter "Household Employer Agent." If you are a trust that qualifies as a household employer, you do not need a separate EIN for reporting tax information relating to household employees; use the EIN of the trust.

● **QSub.** For a qualified subchapter S subsidiary (QSub) check the "Other" box and specify "QSub."

● **Withholding agent.** If you are a withholding agent required to file Form 1042, check the "Other" box and enter "Withholding Agent."

**Sole proprietor.** Check this box if you file Schedule C, C-EZ, or F (Form 1040) and have a qualified plan, or are required to file excise, employment, alcohol, tobacco, or firearms returns, or are a payer of gambling winnings. Enter your SSN (or ITIN) in the space provided. If you are a nonresident alien with no effectively connected income from sources within the United States, you do not need to enter an SSN or ITIN.

**Corporation.** This box is for any corporation **other than a personal service corporation.** If you check this box, enter the income tax form number to be filed by the entity in the space provided.

 *If you entered "1120S" after the "Corporation" checkbox, the corporation **must** file Form 2553 **no later than the 15th day of the 3rd month of the tax year the election is to take effect.** Until Form 2553 has been received and approved, you will be considered a Form 1120 filer. See the Instructions for Form 2553.*

**Personal service corp.** Check this box if the entity is a personal service corporation. An entity is a personal service corporation for a tax year only if:

-3-

• The principal activity of the entity during the testing period (prior tax year) for the tax year is the performance of personal services substantially by employee-owners, and

• The employee-owners own at least 10% of the fair market value of the outstanding stock in the entity on the last day of the testing period.

Personal services include performance of services in such fields as health, law, accounting, or consulting. For more information about personal service corporations, see the Instructions for Forms 1120 and 1120-A and Pub. 542.

**Other nonprofit organization.** Check this box if the nonprofit organization is other than a church or church-controlled organization and specify the type of nonprofit organization (for example, an educational organization).

*If the organization also seeks tax-exempt status, you **must** file either Package 1023 or Package 1024. See Pub. 557 for more information.*

If the organization is covered by a group exemption letter, enter the four-digit **group exemption number (GEN).** (Do not confuse the GEN with the nine-digit EIN.) If you do not know the GEN, contact the parent organization. Get Pub. 557 for more information about group exemption numbers.

**Plan administrator.** If the plan administrator is an individual, enter the plan administrator's SSN in the space provided.

**REMIC.** Check this box if the entity has elected to be treated as a real estate mortgage investment conduit (REMIC). See the Instructions for Form 1066 for more information.

**Limited liability company (LLC).** An LLC is an entity organized under the laws of a state or foreign country as a limited liability company. For Federal tax purposes, an LLC may be treated as a partnership or corporation or be disregarded as an entity separate from its owner.

By **default,** a domestic LLC with only one member is **disregarded** as an entity separate from its owner and must include all of its income and expenses on the owner's tax return (e.g., **Schedule C (Form 1040)**). Also by default, a domestic LLC with two or more members is treated as a partnership. A domestic LLC may file Form 8832 to avoid either default classification and elect to be classified as an association taxable as a corporation. For more information on entity classifications (including the rules for foreign entities), see the instructions for Form 8832.

*Do not file Form 8832 if the LLC accepts the default classifications above. **However, if the LLC will be electing S Corporation status, it must timely file both Form 8832 and Form 2553.***

**Complete Form SS-4 for LLCs as follows:**

• A single-member domestic LLC that accepts the default classification (above) does not need an EIN and generally should not file Form SS-4. Generally, the LLC should use the name and EIN of its **owner** for all Federal tax purposes. However, the reporting and payment of employment taxes for employees of the LLC may be made using the name and EIN of **either** the owner or the LLC as explained in Notice 99-6. You can find Notice 99-6 on page 12 of Internal Revenue Bulletin 1999-3 at **www.irs.gov/pub/irs-irbs/irb99-03.pdf. (Note:** If the LLC applicant indicates in box 13 that it has employees or expects to have employees, the owner (whether an individual or other entity) of a single-member domestic LLC will also be assigned its own EIN (if it does not already have one) even if the LLC will be filing the employment tax returns.)

• A single-member, domestic LLC that accepts the default classification (above) and wants an EIN for filing employment tax returns (see above) or non-Federal purposes, such as a state requirement, must check the "Other" box and write "Disregarded Entity" or, when applicable, "Disregarded Entity—Sole Proprietorship" in the space provided.

• A multi-member, domestic LLC that accepts the default classification (above) must check the "Partnership" box.

• A domestic LLC that will be filing Form 8832 to elect corporate status must check the "Corporation" box and write in "Single-Member" or "Multi-Member" immediately below the "form number" entry line.

**Line 9—Reason for applying.** Check only **one** box. Do not enter "N/A."

**Started new business.** Check this box if you are starting a new business that requires an EIN. If you check this box, enter the type of business being started. **Do not** apply if you already have an EIN and are only adding another place of business.

**Hired employees.** Check this box if the existing business is requesting an EIN because it has hired or is hiring employees and is therefore required to file employment tax returns. **Do not** apply if you already have an EIN and are only hiring employees. For information on employment taxes (e.g., for family members), see Circular E.

*You may be required to make electronic deposits of all depository taxes (such as employment tax, excise tax, and corporate income tax) using the Electronic Federal Tax Payment System (EFTPS). See section 11, Depositing Taxes, of Circular E and Pub. 966.*

**Created a pension plan.** Check this box if you have created a pension plan and need an EIN for reporting purposes. Also, enter the type of plan in the space provided.

*Check this box if you are applying for a trust EIN when a new pension plan is established. In addition, check the "Other" box in line 8a and write "Created a Pension Plan" in the space provided.*

**Banking purpose.** Check this box if you are requesting an EIN for banking purposes only, and enter the banking purpose (for example, a bowling league for depositing dues or an investment club for dividend and interest reporting).

**Changed type of organization.** Check this box if the business is changing its type of organization. For example, the business was a sole proprietorship and has been incorporated or has become a partnership. If you check this box, specify in the space provided (including available space immediately below) the type of change made. For example, "From Sole Proprietorship to Partnership."

**Purchased going business.** Check this box if you purchased an existing business. **Do not** use the former owner's EIN unless you became the "owner" of a corporation by acquiring its stock.

**Created a trust.** Check this box if you created a trust, and enter the type of trust created. For example, indicate if the trust is a nonexempt charitable trust or a split-interest trust.

**Exception.** Do **not** file this form for certain grantor-type trusts. The trustee does not need an EIN for the trust if the trustee furnishes the name and TIN of the grantor/owner and the address of the trust to all payors. See the Instructions for Form 1041 for more information.

 *Do not check this box if you are applying for a trust EIN when a new pension plan is established. Check "Created a pension plan."*

**Other.** Check this box if you are requesting an EIN for any other reason; and enter the reason. For example, a newly-formed state government entity should enter "Newly-Formed State Government Entity" in the space provided.

**Line 10—Date business started or acquired.** If you are starting a new business, enter the starting date of the business. If the business you acquired is already operating, enter the date you acquired the business. If you are changing the form of ownership of your business, enter the date the new ownership entity began. Trusts should enter the date the trust was legally created. Estates should enter the date of death of the decedent whose name appears on line 1 or the date when the estate was legally funded.

**Line 11—Closing month of accounting year.** Enter the last month of your accounting year or tax year. An accounting or tax year is usually 12 consecutive months, either a calendar year or a fiscal year (including a period of 52 or 53 weeks). A calendar year is 12 consecutive months ending on December 31. A fiscal year is either 12 consecutive months ending on the last day of any month other than December or a 52-53 week year. For more information on accounting periods, see Pub. 538.

**Individuals.** Your tax year generally will be a calendar year.

**Partnerships.** Partnerships must adopt one of the following tax years:
- The tax year of the majority of its partners,
- The tax year common to all of its principal partners,
- The tax year that results in the least aggregate deferral of income, or
- In certain cases, some other tax year.

See the Instructions for Form 1065 for more information.

**REMICs.** REMICs must have a calendar year as their tax year.

**Personal service corporations.** A personal service corporation generally must adopt a calendar year unless:
- It can establish a business purpose for having a different tax year, or
- It elects under section 444 to have a tax year other than a calendar year.

**Trusts.** Generally, a trust must adopt a calendar year except for the following:
- Tax-exempt trusts,
- Charitable trusts, and
- Grantor-owned trusts.

**Line 12—First date wages or annuities were paid or will be paid.** If the business has or will have employees, enter the date on which the business began or will begin to pay wages. If the business does not plan to have employees, enter "N/A."

**Withholding agent.** Enter the date you began or will begin to pay income (including annuities) to a nonresident alien. This also applies to individuals who are required to file Form 1042 to report alimony paid to a nonresident alien.

**Line 13—Highest number of employees expected in the next 12 months.** Complete each box by entering the number (including zero ("-0-")) of "Agricultural," "Household," or "Other" employees expected by the applicant in the next 12 months. For a definition of agricultural labor (farmwork), see Circular A.

**Lines 14 and 15.** Check the **one** box in line 14 that best describes the principal activity of the applicant's business. Check the "Other" box (and specify the applicant's principal activity) if none of the listed boxes applies.

Use line 15 to describe the applicant's principal line of business in more detail. For example, if you checked the "Construction" box in line 14, enter additional detail such as "General contractor for residential buildings" in line 15.

**Construction.** Check this box if the applicant is engaged in erecting buildings or other structures, (e.g., streets, highways, bridges, tunnels). The term "Construction" also includes special trade contractors, (e.g., plumbing, HVAC, electrical, carpentry, concrete, excavation, etc. contractors).

**Real estate.** Check this box if the applicant is engaged in renting or leasing real estate to others; managing, selling, buying or renting real estate for others; or providing related real estate services (e.g., appraisal services).

**Rental and leasing.** Check this box if the applicant is engaged in providing tangible goods such as autos, computers, consumer goods, or industrial machinery and equipment to customers in return for a periodic rental or lease payment.

**Manufacturing.** Check this box if the applicant is engaged in the mechanical, physical, or chemical transformation of materials, substances, or components into new products. The assembling of component parts of manufactured products is also considered to be manufacturing.

**Transportation & warehousing.** Check this box if the applicant provides transportation of passengers or cargo; warehousing or storage of goods; scenic or sight-seeing transportation; or support activities related to these modes of transportation.

**Finance & insurance.** Check this box if the applicant is engaged in transactions involving the creation, liquidation, or change of ownership of financial assets and/or facilitating such financial transactions; underwriting annuities/insurance policies; facilitating such underwriting by selling insurance policies; or by providing other insurance or employee-benefit related services.

**Health care and social assistance.** Check this box if the applicant is engaged in providing physical, medical, or psychiatric care using licensed health care professionals or providing social assistance activities such as youth centers, adoption agencies, individual/family services, temporary shelters, etc.

**Accommodation & food services.** Check this box if the applicant is engaged in providing customers with lodging, meal preparation, snacks, or beverages for immediate consumption.

**Wholesale–agent/broker.** Check this box if the applicant is engaged in arranging for the purchase or sale of goods owned by others or purchasing goods on a commission basis for goods traded in the wholesale market, usually between businesses.

**Wholesale–other.** Check this box if the applicant is engaged in selling goods in the wholesale market generally to other businesses for resale on their own account.

**Retail.** Check this box if the applicant is engaged in selling merchandise to the general public from a fixed store; by direct, mail-order, or electronic sales; or by using vending machines.

**Other.** Check this box if the applicant is engaged in an activity not described above. Describe the applicant's principal business activity in the space provided.

**Lines 16a-c.** Check the applicable box in line 16a to indicate whether or not the entity (or individual) applying for an EIN was issued one previously. Complete lines 16b and 16c **only** if the "Yes" box in line 16a is checked. If the applicant previously applied for **more than one** EIN, write "See Attached" in the empty space in line 16a and attach a separate sheet providing the line 16b and 16c information for each EIN previously requested.

**Third Party Designee.** Complete this section **only** if you want to authorize the named individual to receive the entity's EIN and answer questions about the completion of Form SS-4. The designee's authority terminates at the time the EIN is assigned and released to the designee. **You must complete the signature area for the authorization to be valid.**

**Signature.** When required, the application must be signed by **(a)** the individual, if the applicant is an individual, **(b)** the president, vice president, or other principal officer, if the applicant is a corporation, **(c)** a responsible and duly authorized member or officer having knowledge of its affairs, if the applicant is a partnership, government entity, or other unincorporated organization, or **(d)** the fiduciary, if the applicant is a trust or an estate. Foreign applicants may have any duly-authorized person, (e.g., division manager), sign Form SS-4.

**Privacy Act and Paperwork Reduction Act Notice.** We ask for the information on this form to carry out the Internal Revenue laws of the United States. We need it to comply with section 6109 and the regulations thereunder which generally require the inclusion of an employer identification number (EIN) on certain returns, statements, or other documents filed with the Internal Revenue Service. If your entity is required to obtain an EIN, you are required to provide all of the information requested on this form. Information on this form may be used to determine which Federal tax returns you are required to file and to provide you with related forms and publications.

We disclose this form to the Social Security Administration for their use in determining compliance with applicable laws. We may give this information to the Department of Justice for use in civil and criminal litigation, and to the cities, states, and the District of Columbia for use in administering their tax laws. We may also disclose this information to Federal and state agencies to enforce Federal nontax criminal laws and to combat terrorism.

We will be unable to issue an EIN to you unless you provide all of the requested information which applies to your entity. Providing false information could subject you to penalties.

You are not required to provide the information requested on a form that is subject to the Paperwork Reduction Act unless the form displays a valid OMB control number. Books or records relating to a form or its instructions must be retained as long as their contents may become material in the administration of any Internal Revenue law. Generally, tax returns and return information are confidential, as required by section 6103.

The time needed to complete and file this form will vary depending on individual circumstances. The estimated average time is:

| | |
|---|---|
| **Recordkeeping** . . . . . . . . . . . . . . . . . . . . . . . . . | 6 min. |
| **Learning about the law or the form** . . . . . . . . | 22 min. |
| **Preparing the form** . . . . . . . . . . . . . . . . . . . . . | 46 min. |
| **Copying, assembling, and sending the form to the IRS** . . . . . . . . . . . . . . . . . . . . . . . . . . . . | 20 min. |

If you have comments concerning the accuracy of these time estimates or suggestions for making this form simpler, we would be happy to hear from you. You can write to the Tax Products Coordinating Committee, Western Area Distribution Center, Rancho Cordova, CA 95743-0001. **Do not** send the form to this address. Instead, see **How To Apply** on page 1.

Printed on recycled paper

**Form SS-8**
(Rev. June 2003)
Department of the Treasury
Internal Revenue Service

# Determination of Worker Status
## for Purposes of Federal Employment Taxes
## and Income Tax Withholding

OMB No. 1545-0004

| Name of firm (or person) for whom the worker performed services | Worker's name |
|---|---|

Firm's address (include street address, apt. or suite no., city, state, and ZIP code)

Worker's address (include street address, apt. or suite no., city, state, and ZIP code)

| Trade name | Telephone number (include area code) ( ) | Worker's social security number |
|---|---|---|

| Telephone number (include area code) ( ) | Firm's employer identification number | Worker's employer identification number (if any) |
|---|---|---|

If the worker is paid by a firm other than the one listed on this form for these services, enter the name, address, and employer identification number of the payer.

## Important Information Needed To Process Your Request

We must have your permission to disclose your name and the information on this form and any attachments to other parties involved with this request. **Do we have your permission to disclose this information?** . . . . . . . ☐ **Yes** ☐ **No**
If you answered "No" or did not mark a box, we will not process your request and will not issue a determination.

**You must answer ALL items OR mark them "Unknown" or "Does not apply."** If you need more space, attach another sheet.

**A** This form is being completed by: ☐ Firm ☐ Worker; for services performed _____ to _____ .
(beginning date) (ending date)

**B** Explain your reason(s) for filing this form (e.g., you received a bill from the IRS, you believe you received a Form 1099 or Form W-2 erroneously, you are unable to get worker's compensation benefits, you were audited or are being audited by the IRS). ------------------------------
------------------------------
------------------------------
------------------------------

**C** Total number of workers who performed or are performing the same or similar services _____ .

**D** How did the worker obtain the job? ☐ Application ☐ Bid ☐ Employment Agency ☐ Other (specify) _____ .

**E** Attach copies of all supporting documentation (contracts, invoices, memos, Forms W-2, Forms 1099, IRS closing agreements, IRS rulings, etc.). In addition, please inform us of any current or past litigation concerning the worker's status. If no income reporting forms (Form 1099-MISC or W-2) were furnished to the worker, enter the amount of income earned for the year(s) at issue $ _____ .

**F** Describe the firm's business. ------------------------------
------------------------------
------------------------------
------------------------------

**G** Describe the work done by the worker and provide the worker's job title. ------------------------------
------------------------------
------------------------------
------------------------------

**H** Explain why you believe the worker is an employee or an independent contractor. ------------------------------
------------------------------
------------------------------
------------------------------

**I** Did the worker perform services for the firm before getting this position? . . . . . . . . . . . ☐ **Yes** ☐ **No** ☐ **N/A**
If "Yes," what were the dates of the prior service? ------------------------------
If "Yes," explain the differences, if any, between the current and prior service. ------------------------------
------------------------------
------------------------------
------------------------------

**J** If the work is done under a written agreement between the firm and the worker, attach a copy (preferably signed by both parties). Describe the terms and conditions of the work arrangement. ------------------------------

---

**For Privacy Act and Paperwork Reduction Act Notice, see page 5.** Cat. No. 16106T Form **SS-8** (Rev. 6-2003)

## Part I  Behavioral Control

1  What specific training and/or instruction is the worker given by the firm? ...............................................................

2  How does the worker receive work assignments? ...............................................................................................

3  Who determines the methods by which the assignments are performed? ...............................................................

4  Who is the worker required to contact if problems or complaints arise and who is responsible for their resolution? ..........

5  What types of reports are required from the worker? Attach examples. ...............................................................

6  Describe the worker's daily routine (i.e., schedule, hours, etc.). ...............................................................

7  At what location(s) does the worker perform services (e.g., firm's premises, own shop or office, home, customer's location, etc.)? ..........

8  Describe any meetings the worker is required to attend and any penalties for not attending (e.g., sales meetings, monthly meetings, staff meetings, etc.). ...............................................................

9  Is the worker required to provide the services personally? . . . . . . . . . . . . . . . . . . ☐ Yes  ☐ No

10 If substitutes or helpers are needed, who hires them? ...............................................................

11 If the worker hires the substitutes or helpers, is approval required? . . . . . . . . . . . . . ☐ Yes  ☐ No
   If "Yes," by whom? ...............................................................

12 Who pays the substitutes or helpers? ...............................................................

13 Is the worker reimbursed if the worker pays the substitutes or helpers? . . . . . . . . . . . . ☐ Yes  ☐ No
   If "Yes," by whom?

## Part II  Financial Control

1  List the supplies, equipment, materials, and property provided by each party:
   The firm ...............................................................
   The worker ...............................................................
   Other party ...............................................................

2  Does the worker lease equipment? . . . . . . . . . . . . . . . . . . . . . . . . ☐ Yes  ☐ No
   If "Yes," what are the terms of the lease? (Attach a copy or explanatory statement.) ...............................................................

3  What expenses are incurred by the worker in the performance of services for the firm? ...............................................................

4  Specify which, if any, expenses are reimbursed by:
   The firm ...............................................................
   Other party ...............................................................

5  Type of pay the worker receives:  ☐ Salary   ☐ Commission   ☐ Hourly Wage   ☐ Piece Work
   ☐ Lump Sum   ☐ Other (specify) ...............................................................
   If type of pay is commission, and the firm guarantees a minimum amount of pay, specify amount $ _____ .

6  Is the worker allowed a drawing account for advances? . . . . . . . . . . . . . . . . . ☐ Yes  ☐ No
   If "Yes," how often? ...............................................................
   Specify any restrictions. ...............................................................

7  Whom does the customer pay? . . . . . . . . . . . . . . . . . ☐ Firm   ☐ Worker
   If worker, does the worker pay the total amount to the firm? ☐ Yes  ☐ No  If "No," explain. ...............................................................

8  Does the firm carry worker's compensation insurance on the worker? . . . . . . . . . . . . ☐ Yes  ☐ No

9  What economic loss or financial risk, if any, can the worker incur beyond the normal loss of salary (e.g., loss or damage of equipment, material, etc.)? ...............................................................

## Part III — Relationship of the Worker and Firm

**1** List the benefits available to the worker (e.g., paid vacations, sick pay, pensions, bonuses). ------------------------------

**2** Can the relationship be terminated by either party without incurring liability or penalty? . . . . . . . . . . ☐ **Yes**  ☐ **No**
If "No," explain your answer. ------------------------------

**3** Does the worker perform similar services for others? . . . . . . . . . . . . . . . . ☐ **Yes**  ☐ **No**
If "Yes," is the worker required to get approval from the firm? . . . . . . . . . . . . . ☐ **Yes**  ☐ **No**

**4** Describe any agreements prohibiting competition between the worker and the firm while the worker is performing services or during any later period. Attach any available documentation. ------------------------------

**5** Is the worker a member of a union? . . . . . . . . . . . . . . . . . ☐ **Yes**  ☐ **No**

**6** What type of advertising, if any, does the worker do (e.g., a business listing in a directory, business cards, etc.)? Provide copies, if applicable.

**7** If the worker assembles or processes a product at home, who provides the materials and instructions or pattern? ------------

**8** What does the worker do with the finished product (e.g., return it to the firm, provide it to another party, or sell it)? ------------

**9** How does the firm represent the worker to its customers (e.g., employee, partner, representative, or contractor)? ------------

**10** If the worker no longer performs services for the firm, how did the relationship end? ------------

## Part IV — For Service Providers or Salespersons- Complete this part if the worker provided a service directly to customers or is a salesperson.

**1** What are the worker's responsibilities in soliciting new customers? ------------

**2** Who provides the worker with leads to prospective customers? ------------

**3** Describe any reporting requirements pertaining to the leads. ------------

**4** What terms and conditions of sale, if any, are required by the firm? ------------

**5** Are orders submitted to and subject to approval by the firm? . . . . . . . . . . . ☐ **Yes**  ☐ **No**

**6** Who determines the worker's territory? ------------

**7** Did the worker pay for the privilege of serving customers on the route or in the territory? . . . . . . . . . . ☐ **Yes**  ☐ **No**
If "Yes," whom did the worker pay? ------------
If "Yes," how much did the worker pay? . . . . . . . . . . . . $ _____ .

**8** Where does the worker sell the product (e.g., in a home, retail establishment, etc.)? ------------

**9** List the product and/or services distributed by the worker (e.g., meat, vegetables, fruit, bakery products, beverages, or laundry or dry cleaning services). If more than one type of product and/or service is distributed, specify the principal one. ------------

**10** Does the worker sell life insurance full time? . . . . . . . . . . . . . . . ☐ **Yes**  ☐ **No**

**11** Does the worker sell other types of insurance for the firm? . . . . . . . . . . . . ☐ **Yes**  ☐ **No**
If "Yes," enter the percentage of the worker's total working time spent in selling other types of insurance. . . . _____ %

**12** If the worker solicits orders from wholesalers, retailers, contractors, or operators of hotels, restaurants, or other similar establishments, enter the percentage of the worker's time spent in the solicitation. . . . . . . . . . _____ %

**13** Is the merchandise purchased by the customers for resale or use in their business operations? . . . . . . . ☐ **Yes**  ☐ **No**
Describe the merchandise and state whether it is equipment installed on the customers' premises. ------------

## Part V — Signature (see page 4)

Under penalties of perjury, I declare that I have examined this request, including accompanying documents, and to the best of my knowledge and belief, the facts presented are true, correct, and complete.

Signature ▶ _____  Title ▶ _____  Date ▶ _____
    (Type or print name below)

# General Instructions

*Section references are to the Internal Revenue Code unless otherwise noted.*

## Purpose

Firms and workers file Form SS-8 to request a determination of the status of a worker for purposes of Federal employment taxes and income tax withholding.

A Form SS-8 determination may be requested only in order to resolve Federal tax matters. If Form SS-8 is submitted for a tax year for which the statute of limitations on the tax return has expired, a determination letter will not be issued. The statute of limitations expires 3 years from the due date of the tax return or the date filed, whichever is later.

The IRS does not issue a determination letter for proposed transactions or on hypothetical situations. We may, however, issue an information letter when it is considered appropriate.

## Definition

**Firm.** For the purposes of this form, the term "firm" means any individual, business enterprise, organization, state, or other entity for which a worker has performed services. The firm may or may not have paid the worker directly for these services. **If the firm was not responsible for payment for services, be sure to enter the name, address, and employer identification number of the payer on the first page of Form SS-8 below the identifying information for the firm and the worker.**

## The SS-8 Determination Process

The IRS will acknowledge the receipt of your Form SS-8. Because there are usually two (or more) parties who could be affected by a determination of employment status, the IRS attempts to get information from all parties involved by sending those parties blank Forms SS-8 for completion. The case will be assigned to a technician who will review the facts, apply the law, and render a decision. The technician may ask for additional information from the requestor, from other involved parties, or from third parties that could help clarify the work relationship before rendering a decision. The IRS will generally issue a formal determination to the firm or payer (if that is a different entity), and will send a copy to the worker. A determination letter applies only to a worker (or a class of workers) requesting it, and the decision is binding on the IRS. In certain cases, a formal determination will not be issued. Instead, an information letter may be issued. Although an information letter is advisory only and is not binding on the IRS, it may be used to assist the worker to fulfill his or her Federal tax obligations.

Neither the SS-8 determination process nor the review of any records in connection with the determination constitutes an examination (audit) of any Federal tax return. If the periods under consideration have previously been examined, the SS-8 determination process will not constitute a reexamination under IRS reopening procedures. Because this is not an examination of any Federal tax return, the appeal rights available in connection with an examination do not apply to an SS-8 determination. However, if you disagree with a determination and you have additional information concerning the work relationship that you believe was not previously considered, you may request that the determining office reconsider the determination.

## Completing Form SS-8

Answer all questions as completely as possible. Attach additional sheets if you need more space. Provide information for all years the worker provided services for the firm. Determinations are based on the entire relationship between the firm and the worker.

Additional copies of this form may be obtained by calling 1-800-829-4933 or from the IRS website at **www.irs.gov.**

## Fee

There is no fee for requesting an SS-8 determination letter.

## Signature

Form SS-8 must be signed and dated by the taxpayer. A stamped signature will not be accepted.

The person who signs for a corporation must be an officer of the corporation who has personal knowledge of the facts. If the corporation is a member of an affiliated group filing a consolidated return, it must be signed by an officer of the common parent of the group.

The person signing for a trust, partnership, or limited liability company must be, respectively, a trustee, general partner, or member-manager who has personal knowledge of the facts.

## Where To File

Send the completed Form SS-8 to the address listed below for the firm's location. However, for cases involving Federal agencies, send Form SS-8 to the Internal Revenue Service, Attn: CC:CORP:T:C, Ben Franklin Station, P.O. Box 7604, Washington, DC 20044.

| Firm's location: | Send to: |
|---|---|
| Alaska, Arizona, Arkansas, California, Colorado, Hawaii, Idaho, Illinois, Iowa, Kansas, Minnesota, Missouri, Montana, Nebraska, Nevada, New Mexico, North Dakota, Oklahoma, Oregon, South Dakota, Texas, Utah, Washington, Wisconsin, Wyoming, American Samoa, Guam, Puerto Rico, U.S. Virgin Islands | Internal Revenue Service SS-8 Determinations P.O. Box 630 Stop 631 Holtsville, NY 11742-0630 |
| Alabama, Connecticut, Delaware, District of Columbia, Florida, Georgia, Indiana, Kentucky, Louisiana, Maine, Maryland, Massachusetts, Michigan, Mississippi, New Hampshire, New Jersey, New York, North Carolina, Ohio, Pennsylvania, Rhode Island, South Carolina, Tennessee, Vermont, Virginia, West Virginia, all other locations not listed | Internal Revenue Service SS-8 Determinations 40 Lakemont Road Newport, VT 05855-1555 |

## Instructions for Workers

If you are requesting a determination for more than one firm, complete a separate Form SS-8 for each firm.

 *Form SS-8 is not a claim for refund of social security and Medicare taxes or Federal income tax withholding.*

If the IRS determines that you are an employee, you are responsible for filing an amended return for any corrections related to this decision. A determination that a worker is an employee does not necessarily reduce any current or prior tax liability. For more information, call 1-800-829-1040.

**Time for filing a claim for refund.** Generally, you must file your claim for a credit or refund within 3 years from the date your original return was filed or within 2 years from the date the tax was paid, whichever is later.

**Filing Form SS-8 does not prevent the expiration of the time in which a claim for a refund must be filed.** If you are concerned about a refund, and the statute of limitations for filing a claim for refund for the year(s) at issue has not yet expired, you should file **Form 1040X,** Amended U.S. Individual Income Tax Return, to protect your statute of limitations. File a separate Form 1040X for each year.

On the Form 1040X you file, do not complete lines 1 through 24 on the form. Write "Protective Claim" at the top of the form, sign and date it. In addition, you should enter the following statement in Part II, Explanation of Changes to Income, Deductions, and Credits: "Filed Form SS-8 with the Internal Revenue Service Office in (Holtsville, NY; Newport, VT; or Washington, DC; as appropriate). By filing this protective claim, I reserve the right to file a claim for any refund that may be due after a determination of my employment tax status has been completed."

**Filing Form SS-8 does not alter the requirement to timely file an income tax return.** Do not delay filing your tax return in anticipation of an answer to your SS-8 request. In addition, if applicable, do not delay in responding to a request for payment while waiting for a determination of your worker status.

## Instructions for Firms

If a **worker** has requested a determination of his or her status while working for you, you will receive a request from the IRS to complete a Form SS-8. In cases of this type, the IRS usually gives each party an opportunity to present a statement of the facts because any decision will affect the employment tax status of the parties. Failure to respond to this request will not prevent the IRS from issuing a determination letter based on the information he or she has made available so that the worker may fulfill his or her Federal tax obligations. However, the information that you provide is extremely valuable in determining the status of the worker.

If **you** are requesting a determination for a particular class of worker, complete the form for **one** individual who is representative of the class of workers whose status is in question. If you want a written determination for more than one class of workers, complete a separate Form SS-8 for one worker from each class whose status is typical of that class. A written determination for any worker will apply to other workers of the same class if the facts are not materially different for these workers. Please provide a list of names and addresses of all workers potentially affected by this determination.

If you have a reasonable basis for not treating a worker as an employee, you may be relieved from having to pay employment taxes for that worker under section 530 of the 1978 Revenue Act. However, this relief provision cannot be considered in conjunction with a Form SS-8 determination because the determination does not constitute an examination of any tax return. For more information regarding section 530 of the 1978 Revenue Act and to determine if you qualify for relief under this section, you may visit the IRS website at **www.irs.gov**.

**Privacy Act and Paperwork Reduction Act Notice.** We ask for the information on this form to carry out the Internal Revenue laws of the United States. This information will be used to determine the employment status of the worker(s) described on the form. Subtitle C, Employment Taxes, of the Internal Revenue Code imposes employment taxes on wages. Sections 3121(d), 3306(a), and 3401(c) and (d) and the related regulations define employee and employer for purposes of employment taxes imposed under Subtitle C. Section 6001 authorizes the IRS to request information needed to determine if a worker(s) or firm is subject to these taxes. Section 6109 requires you to provide your taxpayer identification number. Neither workers nor firms are required to request a status determination, but if you choose to do so, you must provide the information requested on this form. Failure to provide the requested information may prevent us from making a status determination. If any worker or the firm has requested a status determination and you are being asked to provide information for use in that determination, you are not required to provide the requested information. However, failure to provide such information will prevent the IRS from considering it in making the status determination. Providing false or fraudulent information may subject you to penalties. Routine uses of this information include providing it to the Department of Justice for use in civil and criminal litigation, to the Social Security Administration for the administration of social security programs, and to cities, states, and the District of Columbia for the administration of their tax laws. We may also disclose this information to Federal and state agencies to enforce Federal nontax criminal laws and to combat terrorism. We may provide this information to the affected worker(s) or the firm as part of the status determination process.

You are not required to provide the information requested on a form that is subject to the Paperwork Reduction Act unless the form displays a valid OMB control number. Books or records relating to a form or its instructions must be retained as long as their contents may become material in the administration of any Internal Revenue law. Generally, tax returns and return information are confidential, as required by section 6103.

The time needed to complete and file this form will vary depending on individual circumstances. The estimated average time is: **Recordkeeping,** 22 hrs.; **Learning about the law or the form,** 47 min.; and **Preparing and sending the form to the IRS,** 1 hr., 11 min. If you have comments concerning the accuracy of these time estimates or suggestions for making this form simpler, we would be happy to hear from you. You can write to the Tax Products Coordinating Committee, Western Area Distribution Center, Rancho Cordova, CA 95743-0001. **Do not** send the tax form to this address. Instead, see **Where To File** on page 4.

*This page intentionally blank*

# Form W-4 (2004)

**Purpose.** Complete Form W-4 so that your employer can withhold the correct Federal income tax from your pay. Because your tax situation may change, you may want to refigure your withholding each year.

**Exemption from withholding.** If you are exempt, complete only lines 1, 2, 3, 4, and 7 and sign the form to validate it. Your exemption for 2004 expires February 16, 2005. See **Pub. 505,** Tax Withholding and Estimated Tax.

**Note:** *You cannot claim exemption from withholding if:* **(a)** *your income exceeds $800 and includes more than $250 of unearned income (e.g., interest and dividends) and* **(b)** *another person can claim you as a dependent on their tax return.*

**Basic instructions.** If you are not exempt, complete the **Personal Allowances Worksheet** below. The worksheets on page 2 adjust your withholding allowances based on itemized

deductions, certain credits, adjustments to income, or two-earner/two-job situations. Complete all worksheets that apply. **However, you may claim fewer (or zero) allowances.**

**Head of household.** Generally, you may claim head of household filing status on your tax return only if you are unmarried and pay more than 50% of the costs of keeping up a home for yourself and your dependent(s) or other qualifying individuals. See line **E** below.

**Tax credits.** You can take projected tax credits into account in figuring your allowable number of withholding allowances. Credits for child or dependent care expenses and the child tax credit may be claimed using the **Personal Allowances Worksheet** below. See **Pub. 919,** How Do I Adjust My Tax Withholding? for information on converting your other credits into withholding allowances.

**Nonwage income.** If you have a large amount of nonwage income, such as interest or dividends, consider making estimated tax payments using

**Form 1040-ES,** Estimated Tax for Individuals. Otherwise, you may owe additional tax.

**Two earners/two jobs.** If you have a working spouse or more than one job, figure the total number of allowances you are entitled to claim on all jobs using worksheets from only one Form W-4. Your withholding usually will be most accurate when all allowances are claimed on the Form W-4 for the highest paying job and zero allowances are claimed on the others.

**Nonresident alien.** If you are a nonresident alien, see the **Instructions for Form 8233** before completing this Form W-4.

**Check your withholding.** After your Form W-4 takes effect, use Pub. 919 to see how the dollar amount you are having withheld compares to your projected total tax for 2004. See Pub. 919, especially if your earnings exceed $125,000 (Single) or $175,000 (Married).

**Recent name change?** If your name on line 1 differs from that shown on your social security card, call 1-800-772-1213 to initiate a name change and obtain a social security card showing your correct name.

---

**Personal Allowances Worksheet** (Keep for your records.)

**A**  Enter "1" for **yourself** if no one else can claim you as a dependent . . . . . . . . . . . . . **A** _____

**B**  Enter "1" if:
- You are single and have only one job; or
- You are married, have only one job, and your spouse does not work; or
- Your wages from a second job or your spouse's wages (or the total of both) are $1,000 or less.

**B** _____

**C**  Enter "1" for your **spouse.** But, you may choose to enter "-0-" if you are married and have either a working spouse or more than one job. (Entering "-0-" may help you avoid having too little tax withheld.) . . . . . . . . . **C** _____

**D**  Enter number of **dependents** (other than your spouse or yourself) you will claim on your tax return . . . . . . . **D** _____

**E**  Enter "1" if you will file as **head of household** on your tax return (see conditions under **Head of household** above) . **E** _____

**F**  Enter "1" if you have at least $1,500 of **child or dependent care expenses** for which you plan to claim a credit . . **F** _____

   (**Note:** *Do not include child support payments. See* **Pub. 503,** *Child and Dependent Care Expenses, for details.*)

**G**  **Child Tax Credit** (including additional child tax credit):
- If your total income will be less than $52,000 ($77,000 if married), enter "2" for each eligible child.
- If your total income will be between $52,000 and $84,000 ($77,000 and $119,000 if married), enter "1" for each eligible child plus "1" **additional** if you have four or more eligible children.

**G** _____

**H**  Add lines A through G and enter total here. **Note:** *This may be different from the number of exemptions you claim on your tax return.* ▶ **H** _____

| For accuracy, complete all worksheets that apply. | • If you plan to **itemize or claim adjustments to income** and want to reduce your withholding, see the **Deductions and Adjustments Worksheet** on page 2. |
|---|---|
| | • If you have **more than one job** or are **married and you and your spouse both work** and the combined earnings from all jobs exceed $35,000 ($25,000 if married) see the **Two-Earner/Two-Job Worksheet** on page 2 to avoid having too little tax withheld. |
| | • If **neither** of the above situations applies, **stop here** and enter the number from line H on line 5 of Form W-4 below. |

-------------------- **Cut here and give Form W-4 to your employer. Keep the top part for your records.** --------------------

| Form **W-4** <br> Department of the Treasury <br> Internal Revenue Service | **Employee's Withholding Allowance Certificate** <br> ▶ **Your employer must send a copy of this form to the IRS if: (a) you claim more than 10 allowances or (b) you claim "Exempt" and your wages are normally more than $200 per week.** | OMB No. 1545-0010 <br> 20**04** |
|---|---|---|

| 1  Type or print your first name and middle initial | Last name | | 2  Your social security number |
|---|---|---|---|

| Home address (number and street or rural route) | 3  ☐ Single  ☐ Married  ☐ Married, but withhold at higher Single rate. <br> **Note:** *If married, but legally separated, or spouse is a nonresident alien, check the "Single" box.* |
|---|---|
| City or town, state, and ZIP code | 4  **If your last name differs from that shown on your social security card, check here. You must call 1-800-772-1213 for a new card.** ▶ ☐ |

**5**  Total number of allowances you are claiming (from line **H** above **or** from the applicable worksheet on page 2)   **5** _____

**6**  Additional amount, if any, you want withheld from each paycheck . . . . . . . . . . . . . .   **6** $ _____

**7**  I claim exemption from withholding for 2004, and I certify that I meet **both** of the following conditions for exemption:
- Last year I had a right to a refund of **all** Federal income tax withheld because I had **no** tax liability **and**
- This year I expect a refund of **all** Federal income tax withheld because I expect to have **no** tax liability.

   If you meet both conditions, write "Exempt" here . . . . . . . . . . . . . . ▶  **7** _____

Under penalties of perjury, I certify that I am entitled to the number of withholding allowances claimed on this certificate, or I am entitled to claim exempt status.

**Employee's signature**
(Form is not valid
unless you sign it.) ▶ _____          **Date** ▶ _____

| 8  Employer's name and address (Employer: Complete lines 8 and 10 only if sending to the IRS.) | 9  Office code (optional) | 10  Employer identification number (EIN) |
|---|---|---|

**For Privacy Act and Paperwork Reduction Act Notice, see page 2.**          Cat. No. 10220Q          Form **W-4** (2004)

## Deductions and Adjustments Worksheet

**Note:** *Use this worksheet only if you plan to itemize deductions, claim certain credits, or claim adjustments to income on your 2004 tax return.*

| | | | |
|---|---|---|---|
| **1** | Enter an estimate of your 2004 itemized deductions. These include qualifying home mortgage interest, charitable contributions, state and local taxes, medical expenses in excess of 7.5% of your income, and miscellaneous deductions. (For 2004, you may have to reduce your itemized deductions if your income is over $142,700 ($71,350 if married filing separately). See **Worksheet 3** in Pub. 919 for details.) . . . | **1** | $ |
| **2** | Enter: { $9,700 if married filing jointly or qualifying widow(er) / $7,150 if head of household / $4,850 if single / $4,850 if married filing separately } . . . . . . . . . . . | **2** | $ |
| **3** | **Subtract** line 2 from line 1. If line 2 is greater than line 1, enter "-0-" . . . . . . . | **3** | $ |
| **4** | Enter an estimate of your 2004 adjustments to income, including alimony, deductible IRA contributions, and student loan interest | **4** | $ |
| **5** | **Add** lines 3 and 4 and enter the total. (Include any amount for credits from **Worksheet 7** in Pub. 919) . | **5** | $ |
| **6** | Enter an estimate of your 2004 nonwage income (such as dividends or interest) . . . . . | **6** | $ |
| **7** | **Subtract** line 6 from line 5. Enter the result, but not less than "-0-" . . . . . . . . . | **7** | $ |
| **8** | **Divide** the amount on line 7 by $3,000 and enter the result here. Drop any fraction . . . . . . | **8** | |
| **9** | Enter the number from the **Personal Allowances Worksheet,** line H, page 1 . . . . | **9** | |
| **10** | **Add** lines 8 and 9 and enter the total here. If you plan to use the **Two-Earner/Two-Job Worksheet,** also enter this total on line 1 below. Otherwise, **stop here** and enter this total on Form W-4, line 5, page 1 . | **10** | |

## Two-Earner/Two-Job Worksheet (See **Two earners/two jobs** on page 1.)

**Note:** *Use this worksheet only if the instructions under line H on page 1 direct you here.*

| | | | |
|---|---|---|---|
| **1** | Enter the number from line H, page 1 (or from line 10 above if you used the **Deductions and Adjustments Worksheet**) | **1** | |
| **2** | Find the number in **Table 1** below that applies to the **LOWEST** paying job and enter it here . . . . | **2** | |
| **3** | If line 1 is **more than or equal to** line 2, subtract line 2 from line 1. Enter the result here (if zero, enter "-0-") and on Form W-4, line 5, page 1. **Do not** use the rest of this worksheet . . . . . . . . | **3** | |

**Note:** *If line 1 is **less than** line 2, enter "-0-" on Form W-4, line 5, page 1. Complete lines 4-9 below to calculate the additional withholding amount necessary to avoid a year-end tax bill.*

| | | | |
|---|---|---|---|
| **4** | Enter the number from line 2 of this worksheet . . . . . . . . . . . **4** | | |
| **5** | Enter the number from line 1 of this worksheet . . . . . . . . . . . **5** | | |
| **6** | **Subtract** line 5 from line 4 . . . . . . . . . . . . . . . . . | **6** | |
| **7** | Find the amount in **Table 2** below that applies to the **HIGHEST** paying job and enter it here . . . . | **7** | $ |
| **8** | **Multiply** line 7 by line 6 and enter the result here. This is the additional annual withholding needed . . | **8** | $ |
| **9** | Divide line 8 by the number of pay periods remaining in 2004. For example, divide by 26 if you are paid every two weeks and you complete this form in December 2003. Enter the result here and on Form W-4, line 6, page 1. This is the additional amount to be withheld from each paycheck . . . . . . . . . | **9** | $ |

### Table 1: Two-Earner/Two-Job Worksheet

| Married Filing Jointly | | | Married Filing Jointly | | | All Others | |
|---|---|---|---|---|---|---|---|
| If wages from **HIGHEST** paying job are- | AND, wages from **LOWEST** paying job are- | Enter on line 2 above | If wages from **HIGHEST** paying job are- | AND, wages from **LOWEST** paying job are- | Enter on line 2 above | If wages from **LOWEST** paying job are- | Enter on line 2 above |
| $0 - $40,000 | $0 - $4,000 | 0 | $40,001 and over | 31,001 - 38,000 | 6 | $0 - $6,000 | 0 |
| | 4,001 - 8,000 | 1 | | 38,001 - 44,000 | 7 | 6,001 - 11,000 | 1 |
| | 8,001 - 17,000 | 2 | | 44,001 - 50,000 | 8 | 11,001 - 18,000 | 2 |
| | 17,001 and over | 3 | | 50,001 - 55,000 | 9 | 18,001 - 25,000 | 3 |
| | | | | 55,001 - 65,000 | 10 | 25,001 - 31,000 | 4 |
| $40,001 and over | $0 - $4,000 | 0 | | 65,001 - 75,000 | 11 | 31,001 - 44,000 | 5 |
| | 4,001 - 8,000 | 1 | | 75,001 - 85,000 | 12 | 44,001 - 55,000 | 6 |
| | 8,001 - 15,000 | 2 | | 85,001 - 100,000 | 13 | 55,001 - 70,000 | 7 |
| | 15,001 - 22,000 | 3 | | 100,001 - 115,000 | 14 | 70,001 - 80,000 | 8 |
| | 22,001 - 25,000 | 4 | | 115,001 and over | 15 | 80,001 - 100,000 | 9 |
| | 25,001 - 31,000 | 5 | | | | 100,001 and over | 10 |

### Table 2: Two-Earner/Two-Job Worksheet

| Married Filing Jointly | | All Others | |
|---|---|---|---|
| If wages from **HIGHEST** paying job are- | Enter on line 7 above | If wages from **HIGHEST** paying job are- | Enter on line 7 above |
| $0 - $60,000 | $470 | $0 - $30,000 | $470 |
| 60,001 - 110,000 | 780 | 30,001 - 70,000 | 780 |
| 110,001 - 150,000 | 870 | 70,001 - 140,000 | 870 |
| 150,001 - 270,000 | 1,020 | 140,001 - 320,000 | 1,020 |
| 270,001 and over | 1,090 | 320,001 and over | 1,090 |

| | | |
|---|---|---|
| **ST-9** **SM** | **MASSACHUSETTS DEPARTMENT OF REVENUE** **MONTHLY SALES AND USE TAX RETURN** YOU MUST FILE THIS FORM EVEN THOUGH NO TAX MAY BE DUE. | 1. GROSS SALES | |
| FEDERAL IDENTIFICATION NUMBER | BE SURE THIS RETURN COVERS THE CORRECT PERIOD     FOR MONTH | 2. SALES FOR RESALE/ EXEMPT SALES OR OTHER ADJUSTMENTS | |

**ST-9**

**SM**

**MASSACHUSETTS DEPARTMENT OF REVENUE**

**MONTHLY SALES AND USE TAX RETURN**

YOU MUST FILE THIS FORM EVEN THOUGH NO TAX MAY BE DUE.

FEDERAL IDENTIFICATION NUMBER

BE SURE THIS RETURN COVERS THE CORRECT PERIOD

FOR MONTH

IF ANY INFOR- MATION IS INCORRECT, SEE INSTRUC- TIONS.

☐ Check here if this is a final return.   ☐ Check here if EFT payment.

| No. | Line | Amount |
|---|---|---|
| 1. | GROSS SALES | |
| 2. | SALES FOR RESALE/ EXEMPT SALES OR OTHER ADJUSTMENTS | |
| 2A. | SALES OF MATERIALS, TOOLS AND FUEL | |
| 2B. | SALES OF MACHINERY AND REPLACEMENT PARTS | |
| 3. | TOTAL NONTAXABLE SALES (ADD LINES 2, 2A AND 2B) | |
| 4. | TAXABLE SALES (SUBTRACT LINE 3 FROM LINE 1; ZERO IF NEGATIVE) | |
| 5. | USE TAX PURCHASES | |
| 6. | TOTAL TAXABLE AMOUNT (ADD LINE 4 AND LINE 5) | |
| 7. | TOTAL TAXES (LINE 6 × .05) | |
| 8. | PENALTIES AND INTEREST | |
| 9. | TOTAL AMOUNT DUE (ADD LINE 7 AND LINE 8) | |

Return is due with payment on or before the 20th day of the month following the month indicated above. Make check payable to Commonwealth of Mass. **Mail to: Mass. Dept. of Revenue, PO Box 7039, Boston, MA 02204-7039.**

I declare under the penalties of perjury that this return (including any accompanying schedules and statements) has been examined by me and to the best of my knowledge and belief is a true, correct and complete return.

Signature      Title      Date

**New owners:** *Do not use previous owner's form to file your return. Any change in ownership or organization requires a new registration. You must file a new Form TA-1.*

**Note:** Lines 2A and 2B are for the sales of items becoming part of property sold or used directly in industrial or certain other production. These items are not to be used for income deductions.

52.5M 7/00 00-B02      ♲ *printed on recycled paper*

*This page intentionally blank*

## M-942

## W42

### MASSACHUSETTS DEPARTMENT OF REVENUE
### EMPLOYER'S MONTHLY RETURN OF INCOME TAXES WITHHELD
**YOU MUST FILE THIS FORM EVEN THOUGH NO TAX MAY BE DUE.**

| FEDERAL IDENTIFICATION NUMBER | BE SURE THIS RETURN COVERS THE CORRECT PERIOD | FOR MONTH/YEAR |
|---|---|---|

NUMBER OF EMPLOYEES FROM WHOM TAXES WERE WITHHELD:

IF ANY INFOR-MATION IS INCORRECT, SEE INSTRUC-TIONS.

☐ Check here if this is a final return. ☐ Check here if EFT payment.

| | |
|---|---|
| 1. AMOUNT WITHHELD | |
| 2. ADJUSTMENT FOR PRIOR AMOUNT WITHHELD* | |
| 3. AMOUNT DUE AFTER ADJUST-MENT (NOT LESS THAN "0") | |
| 4. PENALTIES | |
| 5. INTEREST | |
| 6. TOTAL AMOUNT DUE (ADD LINES 3, 4 AND 5) | |

Return is due with payment on or before the 15th day of the month following the month indicated above, except during March, June, September and December — then due the last day of the following month. Make check payable to Commonwealth of Massachusetts. Mail to: **Massachusetts Department of Revenue, PO Box 7038, Boston, MA 02204.**

CHECK HERE IF USING THE BACK OF THIS FORM: ☐

I declare under the penalties of perjury that this return (including any accompanying schedules and statements) has been examined by me and to the best of my knowledge and belief is a true, correct and complete return.

*Explain any adjustment on reverse or it will be disallowed.

Signature      Title      Date

---

**New owners — do not use previous owner's form to file your return. Any change in ownership or organization requires a new registration. You must file a new Form TA-1.**

| LINE 2 ADJUSTMENT INFORMATION | AS REPORTED | CORRECTED | STATE REASON FOR ADJUSTMENT REQUEST: |
|---|---|---|---|
| AMOUNT WITHHELD | | | |
| ADJUSTMENT PRIOR PERIOD | | | |
| AMOUNT PAID | | | |
| REPORTED UNDER FED. IDENT. NO. | | | |
| REPORTING PERIOD IN ERROR | | | |

88M 7/00 00-B02

♻ printed on recycled paper

*This page intentionally blank*

**MASSACHUSETTS
DIVISION OF
UNEMPLOYMENT
ASSISTANCE**

**EMPLOYER STATUS REPORT**

Complete And Return This Form Within 10 days To:
Status Department - 5th Floor
19 Staniford Street
Boston, MA 02114-2589

**PLEASE TYPE OR PRINT CLEARLY IN INK.**

**ALSO COMPLETE REVERSE SIDE.**
**CALL (617) 626-5075 FOR ASSISTANCE.**

**FOR DIVISION USE ONLY**

Emp. No.: _____   Subj. Date: _____

Reason: _____   Qtr.: _____   13th Wk.: _____

No. Employees: _____   Area: _____   Ind.: _____

Rate Yr: _____   NAICS: _____   Aux: _____

Org.: _____

Deter. By: _____

Pred. No.: _____

Pred. Date: _____

Pred. Cd.: _____

ESR Status: _____

Leasing Code: _____

Employer Type: _____

| | Workforce Training Yr./Rate | Contribution Yr./Rate |
|---|---|---|
| 1. | | |
| 2. | | |
| 3. | | |
| 4. | | |
| 5. | | |

Name of employing unit: _____   Trade name: _____

List **ALL** business locations in Massachusetts. If more than one attach a separate sheet.

No. _____ Street (do not use P.O. box number) _____ City _____ State _____ Zip Code

Mailing address: _____   Address where you keep your payroll records: _____

No. _____ St./P.O. box no. _____ City _____ State _____ Zip Code

Business phone: _____   Federal identification no.: _____

Area Code _____ Number

Owner, partners or officers:

| **Name** | **S.S.A. No.** | **Home address** (do not use P.O. box numbers) | **Title** | Are officers compensated for their services? |
|---|---|---|---|---|
| | | | | ☐ Yes   ☐ No |
| | | | | ☐ Yes   ☐ No |
| | | | | ☐ Yes   ☐ No |

Type of organization: ☐ Individual  ☐ Partnership  ☐ Corporation  ☐ Other (specify) _____

If corporation: date incorporated _____ state _____

First date of employment in Massachusetts: _____

Are you a client of an employee leasing company? ☐ Yes   ☐ No

If yes, name of employee leasing company _____

Are you liable for federal unemployment tax?
☐ Yes   ☐ No   1st date of liability _____

Have you previously been subject to the Massachusetts Employment and Training Law?   ☐ Yes   ☐ No

If yes, give account number _____ name _____

Do you hold an exemption from federal income taxes as a non-profit organization described under section 501 (c)(3) of the Internal Revenue Code?   ☐ Yes   ☐ No

If Yes, please attach a copy of your exemption with this report.

Describe nature of your company's business/industry: _____

Specify your principal activity. Name your principal commodity, product or service.

If your main activity in Massachusetts is to provide support services to other locations of your company, please check appropriate box:

☐ Headquarters   ☐ Research   ☐ Warehouse

☐ Computer Center   ☐ Other (specify) _____

Did you acquire the business of a predecessor?   ☐ Yes   ☐ No   If Yes, state:   date acquired: _____

Name of predecessor: _____   Predecessor DUA account number: _____

Did you acquire **ALL** or **PART** of the business of the predecessor?   ☐ ALL   ☐ PART

Acquisition of one of several locations in Massachusetts is considered **PART** of the business.

How acquired?   ☐ Purchase   ☐ Lease   ☐ Franchise   ☐ Other   (explain) _____

Did you acquire the assets of the predecessor's business?   ☐ Yes   ☐ No

Describe those assets acquired:

Describe those assets **NOT** acquired:

Will the predecessor remain in business in Massachusetts?   ☐ Yes   ☐ No   If No, give the date of last payroll: _____

If **Yes**, what is present Massachusetts location of predecessor? _____

_____ Number of Employees: _____

No. _____ Street _____ City _____ State _____ Zip Code

*Commonwealth of Massachusetts*
Form 1110-A Rev. 02-04

**DOMESTIC EMPLOYERS:**

Did you pay $1,000 or more in cash remuneration in any calendar quarter during the current or preceding calendar year for domestic services?　☐ Yes　☐ No

**AGRICULTURAL EMPLOYERS:**

Did you pay $20,000 or more in cash remuneration for agricultural services during any calendar quarter of the current or preceding calendar year?　☐ Yes　☐ No

Did you employ 10 or more individuals on some day in each of 20 calendar weeks, not necessarily consecutive, in either the current or preceding calendar year?　☐ Yes　☐ No

**ALL OTHER EMPLOYERS:**

Did you pay wages of $1,500 or more in any calendar quarter in either the current or preceding calendar year?　☐ Yes　☐ No

Did you employ one or more individuals on some day in each of 13 weeks, not necessarily consecutive, in either the current or preceding calendar year?　☐ Yes　☐ No

If an "OUT OF STATE" employer, did you have a Massachusetts payroll in excess of $200?　☐ Yes　☐ No

List below the number of individuals in your employ in Massachusetts within each calendar week. Include full and part time employees, also paid officers if a corporation. An individual proprietor or a partner should not be counted as an employee. Show total Massachusetts payroll for each calendar quarter.

| RECORD OF MASSACHUSETTS EMPLOYMENT IN CURRENT CALENDAR YEAR | | | | | | ENTER YEAR |
|---|---|---|---|---|---|---|
| | JANUARY | FEBRUARY | MARCH | APRIL | MAY | JUNE |
| Week Ending | | | | | | |
| Number Employed | | | | | | |
| | JULY | AUGUST | SEPTEMBER | OCTOBER | NOVEMBER | DECEMBER |
| Week Ending | | | | | | |
| Number Employed | | | | | | |
| TOTAL WAGES | 1st QTR. $ | | 2nd QTR. $ | | 3rd QTR. $ | 4th QTR. $ |

| RECORD OF MASSACHUSETTS EMPLOYMENT IN PRECEDING CALENDAR YEAR | | | | | | ENTER YEAR _____ |
|---|---|---|---|---|---|---|
| | JANUARY | FEBRUARY | MARCH | APRIL | MAY | JUNE |
| Week Ending | | | | | | |
| Number Employed | | | | | | |
| | JULY | AUGUST | SEPTEMBER | OCTOBER | NOVEMBER | DECEMBER |
| Week Ending | | | | | | |
| Number Employed | | | | | | |
| TOTAL WAGES | 1st QTR. $ | | 2nd QTR. $ | | 3rd QTR. $ | 4th QTR. $ |

| RECORD OF MASSACHUSETTS EMPLOYMENT IN PRECEDING CALENDAR YEAR | | | | | | ENTER YEAR _____ |
|---|---|---|---|---|---|---|
| | JANUARY | FEBRUARY | MARCH | APRIL | MAY | JUNE |
| Week Ending | | | | | | |
| Number Employed | | | | | | |
| | JULY | AUGUST | SEPTEMBER | OCTOBER | NOVEMBER | DECEMBER |
| Week Ending | | | | | | |
| Number Employed | | | | | | |
| TOTAL WAGES | 1st QTR. $ | | 2nd QTR. $ | | 3rd QTR. $ | 4th QTR. $ |

**PREDECESSOR: I hereby certify that all information submitted by the successor is true in accordance with the transfer.**

Signature: _____ Title: _____
　　　　　　　　owner, partner or officer

**THIS REPORT MUST BE SIGNED BY THE OWNER, A PARTNER OR CORPORATE OFFICER**

I certify, under penalties of perjury, that all statements made hereon are true to the best of my knowledge and belief.

Name of employing unit: _____ Date: _____

Signature: _____ Title: _____

1110-A Rev. 02-04

# INDEX

## U

UCC. *See Uniform Commercial Code*
umbrella policy, 63
unemployment compensation, 73, 74, 161
unemployment insurance, 62
Unfair Debt Collection Practices Law, 116
Unfair Sales Act, 118
Uniform Commercial Code, 117
unions, 96
United States Patent and Trademark Office, 24, 29, 120
USPTO. *See United States Patent and Trademark Office*
usury, 115

## V

volunteer experience, 97

## W

Walsh-Healey Public Contracts Act, 95
Worcester Area Chamber of Commerce, 8
Worker Adjustment and Retraining Notification Act, 96
workers' compensation, 61, 62
workers' compensation insurance, 78
working conditions, 97

## Z

zoning, 45, 47, 50

# SPHINX® PUBLISHING ORDER FORM

| BILL TO: | | SHIP TO: | |
|---|---|---|---|
| | | | |
| | | | |
| Phone # | Terms | F.O.B. | Chicago, IL | Ship Date |

**Charge my:** ☐ VISA  ☐ MasterCard  ☐ American Express

☐ **Money Order or Personal Check**

Credit Card Number

Expiration Date

| Qty | ISBN | Title | Retail | Ext. | Qty | ISBN | Title | Retail | Ext. |
|---|---|---|---|---|---|---|---|---|---|
| | | **SPHINX PUBLISHING NATIONAL TITLES** | | | | 1-57248-374-1 | Law School 101 | $16.95 | |
| | 1-57248-363-6 | 101 Complaint Letters That Get Results | $18.95 | | | 1-57248-377-6 | The Law (In Plain English)® for Small Business | $19.95 | |
| | 1-57248-361-X | The 529 College Savings Plan (2E) | $18.95 | | | 1-57248-223-0 | Legal Research Made Easy (3E) | $21.95 | |
| | 1-57248-349-0 | The Antique and Art Collector's Legal Guide | $24.95 | | | 1-57248-165-X | Living Trusts and Other Ways to Avoid Probate (3E) | $24.95 | |
| | 1-57248-347-4 | Attorney Responsibilities & Client Rights | $19.95 | | | 1-57248-186-2 | Manual de Beneficios para el Seguro Social | $18.95 | |
| | 1-57248-148-X | Cómo Hacer su Propio Testamento | $16.95 | | | 1-57248-220-6 | Mastering the MBE | $16.95 | |
| | 1-57248-226-5 | Cómo Restablecer su propio Crédito y Renegociar sus Deudas | $21.95 | | | 1-57248-167-6 | Most Val. Business Legal Forms You'll Ever Need (3E) | $21.95 | |
| | 1-57248-147-1 | Cómo Solicitar su Propio Divorcio | $24.95 | | | 1-57248-360-1 | Most Val. Personal Legal Forms You'll Ever Need (2E) | $26.95 | |
| | 1-57248-166-8 | The Complete Book of Corporate Forms | $24.95 | | | 1-57248-388-1 | The Power of Attorney Handbook (5E) | $22.95 | |
| | 1-57248-353-9 | The Complete Kit to Selling Your Own Home | $18.95 | | | 1-57248-332-6 | Profit from Intellectual Property | $28.95 | |
| | 1-57248-229-X | The Complete Legal Guide to Senior Care | $21.95 | | | 1-57248-329-6 | Protect Your Patent | $24.95 | |
| | 1-57248-391-1 | The Complete Partnership Book | $24.95 | | | 1-57248-385-7 | Quick Cash | $14.95 | |
| | 1-57248-201-X | The Complete Patent Book | $26.95 | | | 1-57248-344-X | Repair Your Own Credit and Deal with Debt (2E) | $18.95 | |
| | 1-57248-369-5 | Credit Smart | $18.95 | | | 1-57248-350-4 | El Seguro Social Preguntas y Respuestas | $16.95 | |
| | 1-57248-163-3 | Crime Victim's Guide to Justice (2E) | $21.95 | | | 1-57248-217-6 | Sexual Harassment: Your Guide to Legal Action | $18.95 | |
| | 1-57248-367-9 | Employees' Rights | $18.95 | | | 1-57248-219-2 | The Small Business Owner's Guide to Bankruptcy | $21.95 | |
| | 1-57248-365-2 | Employer's Rights | $24.95 | | | 1-57248-168-4 | The Social Security Benefits Handbook (3E) | $18.95 | |
| | 1-57248-251-6 | The Entrepreneur's Internet Handbook | $21.95 | | | 1-57248-216-8 | Social Security Q&A | $12.95 | |
| | 1-57248-235-4 | The Entrepreneur's Legal Guide | $26.95 | | | 1-57248-221-4 | Teen Rights | $22.95 | |
| | 1-57248-346-6 | Essential Guide to Real Estate Contracts (2E) | $18.95 | | | 1-57248-366-0 | Tax Smarts for Small Business | $21.95 | |
| | 1-57248-160-9 | Essential Guide to Real Estate Leases | $18.95 | | | 1-57248-335-0 | Traveler's Rights | $21.95 | |
| | 1-57248-254-0 | Family Limited Partnership | $26.95 | | | 1-57248-236-2 | Unmarried Parents' Rights (2E) | $19.95 | |
| | 1-57248-331-8 | Gay & Lesbian Rights | $26.95 | | | 1-57248-362-8 | U.S. Immigration and Citizenship Q&A | $18.95 | |
| | 1-57248-139-0 | Grandparents' Rights (3E) | $24.95 | | | 1-57248-387-3 | U.S. Immigration Step by Step (2E) | $24.95 | |
| | 1-57248-188-9 | Guía de Inmigración a Estados Unidos (3E) | $24.95 | | | 1-57248-392-X | U.S.A. Immigration Guide (5E) | $26.95 | |
| | 1-57248-187-0 | Guía de Justicia para Víctimas del Crimen | $21.95 | | | 1-57248-192-7 | The Visitation Handbook | $18.95 | |
| | 1-57248-253-2 | Guía Esencial para los Contratos de Arrendamiento de Bienes Raíces | $22.95 | | | 1-57248-225-7 | Win Your Unemployment Compensation Claim (2E) | $21.95 | |
| | 1-57248-103-X | Help Your Lawyer Win Your Case (2E) | $14.95 | | | 1-57248-330-X | The Wills, Estate Planning and Trusts Legal Kit | $26.95 | |
| | 1-57248-334-2 | Homeowner's Rights | $19.95 | | | 1-57248-138-2 | Winning Your Personal Injury Claim (2E) | $24.95 | |
| | 1-57248-164-1 | How to Buy a Condominium or Townhome (2E) | $19.95 | | | 1-57248-333-4 | Working with Your Homeowners Association | $19.95 | |
| | 1-57248-328-8 | How to Buy Your First Home | $18.95 | | | 1-57248-380-6 | Your Right to Child Custody, Visitation and Support (3E) | $24.95 | |
| | 1-57248-191-9 | How to File Your Own Bankruptcy (5E) | $21.95 | | | | **CALIFORNIA TITLES** | | |
| | 1-57248-343-1 | How to File Your Own Divorce (5E) | $26.95 | | | 1-57248-150-1 | CA Power of Attorney Handbook (2E) | $18.95 | |
| | 1-57248-222-2 | How to Form a Limited Liability Company (2E) | $24.95 | | | 1-57248-337-7 | How to File for Divorce in CA (4E) | $26.95 | |
| | 1-57248-231-1 | How to Form a Nonprofit Corporation (2E) | $24.95 | | | 1-57248-145-5 | How to Probate and Settle an Estate in CA | $26.95 | |
| | 1-57248-345-8 | How to Form Your Own Corporation (4E) | $26.95 | | | 1-57248-336-9 | How to Start a Business in CA (2E) | $21.95 | |
| | 1-57248-232-X | How to Make Your Own Simple Will (3E) | $18.95 | | | 1-57248-194-3 | How to Win in Small Claims Court in CA (2E) | $18.95 | |
| | 1-57248-379-2 | How to Register Your Own Copyright (5E) | $24.95 | | | 1-57248-246-X | Make Your Own CA Will | $18.95 | |
| | 1-57248-104-8 | How to Register Your Own Trademark (3E) | $21.95 | | | 1-57248-397-0 | The Landlord's Legal Guide in CA (2E) | $24.95 | |
| | 1-57248-394-6 | How to Write Your Own Living Will (4E) | $18.95 | | | 1-57248-241-9 | Tenants' Rights in CA | $21.95 | |
| | 1-57248-156-0 | How to Write Your Own Premarital Agreement (3E) | $24.95 | | | **Form Continued on Following Page** | | **SubTotal** | |
| | 1-57248-230-3 | Incorporate in Delaware from Any State | $26.95 | | | | | | |
| | 1-57248-158-7 | Incorporate in Nevada from Any State | $24.95 | | | | | | |
| | 1-57248-250-8 | Inmigración a los EE.UU. Paso a Paso | $22.95 | | | | | | |
| | 1-57248-400-4 | Inmigración y Ciudadanía en los EE.UU. Preguntas y Respuestas | $16.95 | | | | | | |

To order, call Sourcebooks at 1-800-432-7444 or FAX (630) 961-2168 (Bookstores, libraries, wholesalers—please call for discount)

*Prices are subject to change without notice.*

Find more legal information at: **www.SphinxLegal.com**

# SPHINX® PUBLISHING ORDER FORM

| Qty | ISBN | Title | Retail | Ext. |
|---|---|---|---|---|
| | | **FLORIDA TITLES** | | |
| ___ | 1-57071-363-4 | Florida Power of Attorney Handbook (2E) | $16.95 | ___ |
| ___ | 1-57248-396-2 | How to File for Divorce in FL (8E) | $28.95 | ___ |
| ___ | 1-57248-356-3 | How to Form a Corporation in FL (6E) | $24.95 | ___ |
| ___ | 1-57248-203-6 | How to Form a Limited Liability Co. in FL (2E) | $24.95 | ___ |
| ___ | 1-57071-401-0 | How to Form a Partnership in FL | $22.95 | ___ |
| ___ | 1-57248-113-7 | How to Make a FL Will (6E) | $16.95 | ___ |
| ___ | 1-57248-088-2 | How to Modify Your FL Divorce Judgment (4E) | $24.95 | ___ |
| ___ | 1-57248-354-7 | How to Probate and Settle an Estate in FL (5E) | $26.95 | ___ |
| ___ | 1-57248-339-3 | How to Start a Business in FL (7E) | $21.95 | ___ |
| ___ | 1-57248-204-4 | How to Win in Small Claims Court in FL (7E) | $18.95 | ___ |
| ___ | 1-57248-381-4 | Land Trusts in Florida (7E) | $29.95 | ___ |
| ___ | 1-57248-338-5 | Landlords' Rights and Duties in FL (9E) | $22.95 | ___ |
| | | **GEORGIA TITLES** | | |
| ___ | 1-57248-340-7 | How to File for Divorce in GA (5E) | $21.95 | ___ |
| ___ | 1-57248-180-3 | How to Make a GA Will (4E) | $16.95 | ___ |
| ___ | 1-57248-341-5 | How to Start a Business in Georgia (3E) | $21.95 | ___ |
| | | **ILLINOIS TITLES** | | |
| ___ | 1-57248-244-3 | Child Custody, Visitation, and Support in IL | $24.95 | ___ |
| ___ | 1-57248-206-0 | How to File for Divorce in IL (3E) | $24.95 | ___ |
| ___ | 1-57248-170-6 | How to Make an IL Will (3E) | $16.95 | ___ |
| ___ | 1-57248-247-8 | How to Start a Business in IL (3E) | $21.95 | ___ |
| ___ | 1-57248-252-4 | The Landlord's Legal Guide in IL | $24.95 | ___ |
| | | **MARYLAND, VIRGINIA AND THE DISTRICT OF COLUMBIA** | | |
| ___ | 1-57248-240-0 | How to File for Divorce in MD, VA and DC | $28.95 | ___ |
| ___ | 1-57248-359-8 | How to Start a Business in MD, VA or DC | $21.95 | ___ |
| | | **MASSACHUSETTS TITLES** | | |
| ___ | 1-57248-128-5 | How to File for Divorce in MA (3E) | $24.95 | ___ |
| ___ | 1-57248-115-3 | How to Form a Corporation in MA | $24.95 | ___ |
| ___ | 1-57248-108-0 | How to Make a MA Will (2E) | $16.95 | ___ |
| ___ | 1-57248-248-6 | How to Start a Business in MA (3E) | $21.95 | ___ |
| ___ | 1-57248-398-9 | The Landlord's Legal Guide in MA (2E) | $24.95 | ___ |
| | | **MICHIGAN TITLES** | | |
| ___ | 1-57248-215-X | How to File for Divorce in MI (3E) | $24.95 | ___ |
| ___ | 1-57248-182-X | How to Make a MI Will (3E) | $16.95 | ___ |
| ___ | 1-57248-183-8 | How to Start a Business in MI (3E) | $18.95 | ___ |
| | | **MINNESOTA TITLES** | | |
| ___ | 1-57248-142-0 | How to File for Divorce in MN | $21.95 | ___ |
| ___ | 1-57248-179-X | How to Form a Corporation in MN | $24.95 | ___ |
| ___ | 1-57248-178-1 | How to Make a MN Will (2E) | $16.95 | ___ |
| | | **NEW JERSEY TITLES** | | |
| ___ | 1-57248-239-7 | How to File for Divorce in NJ | $24.95 | ___ |
| ___ | 1-57248-448-9 | How to Start a Business in NJ | $21.95 | ___ |
| | | **NEW YORK TITLES** | | |
| ___ | 1-57248-193-5 | Child Custody, Visitation and Support in NY | $26.95 | ___ |
| ___ | 1-57248-351-2 | File for Divorce in NY | $26.95 | ___ |
| ___ | 1-57248-249-4 | How to Form a Corporation in NY (2E) | $24.95 | ___ |
| ___ | 1-57248-401-2 | How to Make a NY Will (3E) | $16.95 | ___ |
| ___ | 1-57248-199-4 | How to Start a Business in NY (2E) | $18.95 | ___ |
| ___ | 1-57248-198-6 | How to Win in Small Claims Court in NY (2E) | $18.95 | ___ |
| ___ | 1-57248-197-8 | Landlords' Legal Guide in NY | $24.95 | ___ |
| ___ | 1-57071-188-7 | New York Power of Attorney Handbook | $19.95 | ___ |

| Qty | ISBN | Title | Retail | Ext. |
|---|---|---|---|---|
| ___ | 1-57248-122-6 | Tenants' Rights in NY | $21.95 | ___ |
| | | **NORTH CAROLINA TITLES** | | |
| ___ | 1-57248-185-4 | How to File for Divorce in NC (3E) | $22.95 | ___ |
| ___ | 1-57248-129-3 | How to Make a NC Will (3E) | $16.95 | ___ |
| ___ | 1-57248-184-6 | How to Start a Business in NC (3E) | $18.95 | ___ |
| ___ | 1-57248-091-2 | Landlords' Rights & Duties in NC | $21.95 | ___ |
| | | **NORTH CAROLINA AND SOUTH CAROLINA TITLES** | | |
| ___ | 1-57248-371-7 | How to Start a Business in NC or SC | $24.95 | ___ |
| | | **OHIO TITLES** | | |
| ___ | 1-57248-190-0 | How to File for Divorce in OH (2E) | $24.95 | ___ |
| ___ | 1-57248-174-9 | How to Form a Corporation in OH | $24.95 | ___ |
| ___ | 1-57248-173-0 | How to Make an OH Will | $16.95 | ___ |
| | | **PENNSYLVANIA TITLES** | | |
| ___ | 1-57248-242-7 | Child Custody, Visitation and Support in PA | $26.95 | ___ |
| ___ | 1-57248-211-7 | How to File for Divorce in PA (3E) | $26.95 | ___ |
| ___ | 1-57248-358-X | How to Form a Cooporation in PA | $24.95 | ___ |
| ___ | 1-57248-094-7 | How to Make a PA Will (2E) | $16.95 | ___ |
| ___ | 1-57248-357-1 | How to Start a Business in PA (3E) | $21.95 | ___ |
| ___ | 1-57248-245-1 | The Landlord's Legal Guide in PA | $24.95 | ___ |
| | | **TEXAS TITLES** | | |
| ___ | 1-57248-171-4 | Child Custody, Visitation, and Support in TX | $22.95 | ___ |
| ___ | 1-57248-399-7 | How to File for Divorce in TX (4E) | $24.95 | ___ |
| ___ | 1-57248-114-5 | How to Form a Corporation in TX (2E) | $24.95 | ___ |
| ___ | 1-57248-255-9 | How to Make a TX Will (3E) | $16.95 | ___ |
| ___ | 1-57248-214-1 | How to Probate and Settle an Estate in TX (3E) | $26.95 | ___ |
| ___ | 1-57248-228-1 | How to Start a Business in TX (3E) | $18.95 | ___ |
| ___ | 1-57248-111-0 | How to Win in Small Claims Court in TX (2E) | $16.95 | ___ |
| ___ | 1-57248-355-5 | The Landlord's Legal Guide in TX | $24.95 | ___ |

SubTotal This page ___

SubTotal previous page ___

Shipping — $5.00 for 1st book, $1.00 each additional ___

Illinois residents add 6.75% sales tax ___

Connecticut residents add 6.00% sales tax ___

**Total** ___

To order, call Sourcebooks at 1-800-432-7444 or FAX (630) 961-2168 (Bookstores, libraries, wholesalers—please call for discount)

*Prices are subject to change without notice.*

Find more legal information at: **www.SphinxLegal.com**